LIFE IN
ROMAN
LONDON

LIFE IN ROMAN LONDON

SIMON WEBB

The
History
Press

First published 2011

The History Press
The Mill, Brimscombe Port
Stroud, Gloucestershire, GL5 2QG
www.thehistorypress.co.uk

British Library Cataloguing in Publication Data.
A catalogue record for this book is available from the British Library.

ISBN 978 0 7524 6536 4

Typesetting and origination by The History Press
Printed in the EU for The History Press.

Contents

Introduction

This is the story of Roman London. The aim of this book is to explain what life was like for people living in London between the invasion of Britain in AD 43 and the final abandonment of the city something over 400 years later. This is roughly the same length of time as from the execution of Sir Walter Raleigh in the early seventeenth century to the present day; it covers a very long period and to talk of 'Roman London' is meaningless unless the century and sometimes the decade is specified. After all, life in London during the seventeenth century was very different from life now during the early twenty-first century! The same applies to Roman London when comparing the way things were in the late first century with how they were in the early fifth century. During that time, the city was not static, but constantly expanded and shrank, mutated into different forms and changed its identity; not once but a number of times. Our mental image of Roman London is often a snapshot of some reconstruction which owes more to classical Rome than it does to the busy, cosmopolitan port and trading centre that was Londinium. Life in a provincial city such as London was very different from life in Rome itself and it also varied dramatically from one century to another.

Many books on this subject are crammed with the Latin names of important Romans and their settlements and also contain lists of Celtic tribes, together with their leaders. This can be very off-putting for readers. They are forced to plough through references to all sorts of notable people and obscure places, the names of which they cannot even pronounce and will forget as soon as the page is turned. One has to remember, for example, the Dumnonii, who controlled Cornwall and Devon, being careful of course not to confuse them with the Damnonii who were in

Scotland. It is important not to muddle Cogidubnus up with Togdumnus and to remember that it was Tincommius who first succeeded his father Commius the Younger, rather than either of his brothers Eppillus or Verica. It is unlikely in the extreme that most of us will recall any of these names a week after we finish the book.

The effect of being constantly bombarded by dozens of unfamiliar names in this way can be to leave one feeling a little dazed and bewildered. All too often, the effort of struggling through pages and pages of this sort of thing makes reading books about Roman history a worthy chore rather than a relaxing pleasure; for that reason alone, it makes sense to be a little sparing with the use of unaccustomed names, both of people and of places. Wherever possible in the present book, proper names will be avoided and reference made only to the position of the individual concerned: 'the governor of the province', for instance, rather than Suetonius Paulinus or 'a British chieftain' instead of Prasutagus. Some names, Boudica and Julius Caesar for example, are sufficiently well known that readers will recognise them at once. Avoiding the use of the names of such famous historical characters would be mere affectation. An appendix at the back of this book contains brief biographical details of named individuals. It seems to me better to place this information in a separate place, rather than constantly interrupting the main text with notes and explanations.

The same consideration has led to the use of the modern English names of cities and regions throughout this book. Most of us are aware that the Latin name for London was Londinium and many people also know that St Albans was known as Verulamium. I doubt though that many readers will recognise Noviomagus Reginorum as Chichester, nor realise that Exeter was called Isca Dumnoniorum. Similarly, when we read of a Roman campaign in the territory of the Ordovices and Silures, it would probably be easier if we simply thought of this as a military action in Wales. I am aware that this may lead to the occasional appearance of anachronism; this seems to me a price worth paying for the increased clarity produced by such a practice.

There is another good reason for steering clear of too many personal names. The people mentioned in this way tend almost invariably to be governors and kings, statesmen and tribal chiefs. This book is about the London of ordinary people, the mass of men and women who lived and worked in the city, rather than the few who ruled over it. These early Londoners did not in general live in marble palaces with mosaics on the floor and frescos on the walls. The typical book about Roman Britain thus unintentionally gives a distorted perspective of the period. It is rather as though a couple of thousand years from now, some archaeologist were to reconstruct early twenty-first-century London by examining the remains of Buckingham Palace, the site of St Paul's Cathedral and what is left of the Tower of London. Combining this with a few garbled anecdotes from the lives of the Duke of Edinburgh, the Archbishop of Canterbury and perhaps a prime minister or two, he attempts to write the definitive biography of the London of our own time.

This may sound too absurd for words, but it is what often happens when people are writing about Roman history. We see pictures of the amphitheatres and palaces, read about some high-ranking soldiers and a few emperors, then feel that we have been learning about the history of this or that city. Museums all too often encourage this view of the past. Reconstructions of rooms from the Roman occupation of Britain almost invariably show the second-century equivalent of a celebrity home from *Hello* magazine, instead of the ordinary households in which the majority of the population lived.

To make any sense of the lives of people in London at that time, it will first be necessary to see why there was a city in that part of the Thames valley in the first place. In order to discover this, we shall begin our story with the second most memorable date in British history: 55 BC, the year that Julius Caesar first landed in Kent.

A City is Founded

Over 80 years after the book was first published, the opening sentence of *1066 and All That*, by W.C. Sellar and R.J. Yeatman, still retains its power to amuse: 'The first date in English History is 55 BC, in which year Julius Caesar (the memorable Roman emperor) landed, like all other successful invaders of these islands, at Thanet.' It is funny while being at the same time perfectly true; history begins with written records and before Caesar's first landing in Britain we cannot speak with confident knowledge of any event which took place in this country. This first sentence of one of the classics of twentieth-century English humour also contains another broadly true statement which is, as we shall later see, greatly germane to the story of London.

This is a history of the Roman city of Londinium, from which evolved our own city of London. Since it is generally agreed that there was no city in the area before the Roman invasion, it seems reasonable to begin by asking what the Romans were doing here in the first place. How and why did they come to be founding cities in this country? Britain was, after all, a long way from Italy. What first put it into the heads of Roman leaders 2000 years ago to come and conquer this country? Caratacus, the captured British chieftain, summed up this puzzle after he had been deported to Rome following his defeat. He looked around at the beautiful temples and palaces, asking in bewilderment, 'And when you have all this, do you still envy us our hovels?' Others have shared Caratacus' bewilderment over the years and we shall in this chapter try to explore some possible explanations for the presence of Roman legions in this country. Only then will we be asking ourselves why, having established themselves in this island, they chose one particular spot in the Thames valley to build what was to become a mighty walled city, with the largest basilica north of the Alps.

The two questions posed above are very different. The motives for coming to Britain in the first place are complex; there was not one overriding reason for doing so. As to why the city of Londinium was built where it was, this is an easier question to answer, only half a dozen sentences are required to state the case for the location of modern London in that place on the banks of that particular river.

In 55 BC, Julius Caesar landed in Britain at the head of 10,000 soldiers. He stayed for a very short time, left and returned the following year. During this second expedition, he ventured a considerable distance inland, probably crossing the Thames near Westminster and assaulting a fortified settlement in Hertfordshire. He then left Britain for good and it was almost a hundred years before a Roman army landed again on these shores.

Why did Caesar come to Britain? According to his own account, the reason was quite straightforward. Writing in *The Gallic War*, he says, referring to himself rather disconcertingly to modern ears in the third person: 'Caesar made active preparations for an expedition to Britain, because he knew that in almost all the Gallic campaigns the Gauls had received reinforcements from the Britons.' In other words, Caesar presents the matter as a purely military one of an independent area that represented a threat, or more probably merely a serious nuisance, to Roman supremacy in Western Europe.

There is no reason to doubt that Caesar was telling the truth, or at least part of the truth, about his motives in landing an army in this country. Having subdued Gaul, which corresponded roughly to modern-day France, Holland, Belgium and Switzerland, he realised that those fleeing the Roman forces could easily seek shelter in Britain, where they might perhaps be able to regroup. This actually happened after a rebellion against Rome in 57 BC. The following year, when the tribes of Armorica (present-day Brittany) revolted against Rome, the British were swift to send assistance to their fellow Celts. Caesar also knew that Britain was the home and power base of Druidism, a religion which inspired the tribesman of Gaul to resist Roman rule. Was all this enough to justify assembling a fleet of ships and transporting thousands of troops to unknown territory, as Caesar did in 55 BC? The logistics of these expeditions are staggering, even by today's standards; in 54 BC over 600 ships crossed the Channel for Caesar's second invasion. However, just as with wars and invasions today, there were other factors at work leading to the intervention in another country's affairs, quite apart from those given by the military commander on the ground.

In our own time, for instance, there are persistent suggestions that European and American involvement in the Middle East is motivated less by an idealistic commitment to the principles of democracy and more by our need for the mineral resources, primarily oil, which lie beneath the sands of those distant countries to which we dispatch military forces. Could a desire for British material resources have been at the back of the Roman interest in the British Isles? It is possible but unlikely. Although it is true that Britain had large reserves of tin, a most useful metal in antiquity, in Cornwall, the Romans had already secured their own supply in Spain. Strabo, the geographer, writing at about the time of Christ, details some of the things which Britain exported before they became a Roman province. These include tin, iron, slaves, corn, cattle and hides. It is a meagre enough list, containing nothing that would make the occupation of Britain a viable business proposition. In fact, after discussing British exports, Strabo states plainly that it would not be profitable to make Britain a province of Rome, because the revenue from taxes would not be sufficient to pay for the garrison which such a province would require.

On the other hand, writing of Britain in the first century AD, Tacitus says that 'the earth yields gold, silver and other metals; the rewards of victory'. This suggests that there was a feeling among Romans that this country had sufficient mineral resources to make it worth conquering. Most of the gold, which the Britons turned into torcs and other jewellery, did not in fact come from England and Wales, which comprised the province of Britannia, but was acquired by trade from Ireland and Scotland. The story was apparently current though in Rome, that Britain was full of silver and gold and one wonders if this was a rumour which had been circulated by those with a vested interest in the acquisition by Rome of a new province. Who might wish to promote such an idea, that Britain was some species of El Dorado, with abundant supplies of precious metals to be found? The senate had already declared that colonisation by Rome should be limited to the countries around the rim of the Mediterranean. They were opposed in this view by the merchants and businessmen of Rome, who were eager to open up new markets and find new areas to exploit. It is quite possible such men found it worth spreading the story of untold riches awaiting those who colonised Britain.

There were useful metals to be dug out of the ground in Britain, but not in the vast quantities that some apparently believed or purported to believe. There was very little gold, except for small quantities in Wales, but there was lead and mixed in with the lead ore was quite a bit of silver. Britain also has extensive reserves of iron and a fair amount of copper.

A century after Caesar's invasion of Britain, the emperor Claudius invaded the country and it became a province of Rome for the next 400 years or so. Both Caesar and Claudius were in desperate need, at the time of their invasions of Britain, of significant military triumphs. Here lies another, less obvious motive for bringing powerful armies to subdue the tribes of Britain. For two very different reasons, the military commander Caesar and the emperor Claudius wished to demonstrate their martial prowess and found in the island of Britain a handy place to do so.

In Caesar's case, his position before the invasion was a precarious one. His ambitions had made for him powerful enemies back in Rome and there were moves afoot to prosecute him. In 55 BC, the Roman Republic was on the very cusp of changing to an imperial style of government. Powerful individuals like Caesar and Pompey had armies under their control, armies which owed personal allegiance to their commanders rather than to the Roman senate. The government in Rome, composed in the main of idealists, was within a few years to learn that uncomfortable truth which a great twentieth-century leader summed up succinctly as: 'Political power grows from the barrel of a gun.' Mao Tse Tung was not of course the first to realise this, but seldom has the concept been so neatly encapsulated in such a pithy aphorism.

Five years after the second expedition to Britain, Caesar led his army across the Rubicon and eventually seized control of Rome. This struggle between a legitimate, high-minded government and brute, martial force reminds one irresistibly of the occasion during the English Civil War when the king was being held by Parliament. A soldier, Cornet George Joyce, arrived at the house where King Charles was being held and took him into military custody. When the king asked Cornet Joyce indignantly upon what authority he and his troop of cavalry were acting, Joyce replied by drawing his pistol and showing it to the king.

Julius Caesar needed to reinforce his reputation as a ruthless and able military leader, whom it would be unwise to cross. Britain provided a magnificent opportunity for an eye-catching exploit which demonstrated that here was a man who would stop at nothing; a man who was prepared to take his men to the edge of the world and beyond! According to Greek mythology, much of which had been adopted by the Romans, the Earth was encircled by a mighty river called Oceanus. The world at that time was supposed to consist of the Mediterranean Sea and the lands around it:

Greece, Egypt, Italy and so on. When seafarers ventured beyond the Straits of Gibraltar, the Pillars of Hercules as they were then known, some thought that the vast body of water that they encountered was the river of Oceanus and that this was really the edge of the world. By playing on this old myth, Caesar showed himself a man to be reckoned with; a military leader extending Rome's influence to the ancient equivalent of outer space.

Of course, in one sense this was all a lot of nonsense. Merchants had been travelling to and from Britain for centuries, bartering with the inhabitants on a regular basis. The Phoenicians knew Britain well enough and so did many Roman traders who plied the Atlantic coast. But for a number of educated people in Rome, Britain was still an almost legendary place, rather like Atlantis. Some of Cicero's friends didn't believe that it even existed.

For Claudius, the motive for landing forces in Britain was a little different from Caesar's. Here was a man who was installed as emperor by military power and who could, as he knew only too well, be removed in the same way. There were two sound reasons for his wishing to incorporate Britain into the Roman Empire. First, he had been on the throne for two years and wished to make his mark; prove to those around him that he was not a mere puppet or stop-gap leader of the empire. Secondly, he had the example of Julius Caesar to show the perils of allowing too large an army to be concentrated in one place under the leadership of a charismatic figure. Claudius did not want any adventurer to march on Rome as Caesar had done. A good way of preventing this was to split great armies into smaller units and then separate them from each other geographically. Placing 40,000 or so soldiers across the sea in a wild and untamed land would be an excellent means of ensuring that those men at least did not have the leisure to plot a coup d'état against their emperor. Twenty-five years later, Claudius was shown to have been far-sighted and shrewd in his decision to transfer forces to Britain, thus reducing the size of the army in Europe. In AD 69, a commander on the Rhine precipitated a minor civil war. Just as Claudius had feared, when such armies grew too large those in charge of them sometimes tended to become ambitious.

Claudius was handed a ready-made *casus belli* when a minor British king was driven from his territory and appealed to Rome for assistance. In AD 43, he dispatched an army 40,000 strong to conquer Britain. As a matter of fact, he had greater and more genuine strategic reasons for taking this step than Caesar had done. Raids were being launched from Britain against Roman-occupied Europe. Guarding against such raids, should they have increased, would have needed an estimated 40,000 or perhaps 50,000 additional troops stationed on the coast facing the North Sea and English Channel. Not only would any increase in numbers of soldiers create the logistical problem of feeding the men from the existing agricultural system, it would also have massively increased the size of the army in this part of the empire which, for reasons at which we have looked, was thought by Claudius to be undesirable. Moving this many soldiers to Britain would be the ideal solution; they would be fed from the produce of the British countryside.

At his death in AD 14, the emperor Augustus had left posthumous instructions that the empire should not be further enlarged. He had several motives for issuing this prohibition. One was that it secured his place in history as the man who had brought the Roman Empire to its greatest extent. This would indeed be something upon which to reflect with satisfaction on his deathbed. There was too a practical reason why Augustus felt that the empire was now large enough. With no means of communication faster than a galloping horse, maintaining contact between a ruler and his subjects, some of whom live thousands of miles away, could be a lengthy and uncertain business. If an empire grows too large, it becomes unwieldy and sometimes has a tendency to fragment of its own accord. This indeed happened in the later years of the Roman Empire.

One final consideration is that it is in the nature of all great empires to either wax or wane. The empire that tries simply to stay the same size and make no further territorial gains will soon find its borders shrinking as they are nibbled away by greedy, jealous rivals or discontented subject peoples. A conservative policy of non-expansion can easily be mistaken for weakness and so in order to thrive and maintain self-respect, most empires pursue a policy of gobbling up any little lands upon their borders. Thucydides, an author with whom Claudius was certainly familiar, said: 'empires cannot remain stagnant; they must grow, and the managers of empire must pursue growth and keep order with a businesslike disregard for the moral principles they would otherwise hold dear.' This is one more reason for the invasion of Britain 2000 years ago; we were perilously close to a vigorous empire whose leaders wished to show at intervals that they were still a force to be reckoned with.

Ultimately, of course, the Romans needed neither excuse nor justification for their seizure of new territory. Their view of the world echoes the supreme confidence of the white settlers in America and Europeans in Africa during the nineteenth century. Expanding into other lands, occupied only by illiterate savages, was their manifest destiny. It was so plainly the correct and natural way of the world, for civilised people to take their culture to the unenlightened, that it would have been absurd to question the propriety of such an action. That they were Romans and that these other lands were full of barbarians was sufficient justification in itself.

Various factors brought Roman armies to this country. Were the motives that led the invaders to select a certain point along the Thames valley for what was to become the greatest city in Britain similarly complex? By no means. In fact the reason for Londinium growing where London stands today can essentially be summed up in five words: ford and deep-water anchorage. Before we expand a little on this idea, perhaps we should look at what sort of country it was that the Romans visited in 55 BC and later occupied in AD 43. We shall examine particularly closely the Thames valley at that time.

When Julius Caesar landed in Britain, he found a country divided up into various tribal districts. Some of these tribes had been living in Britain for centuries, others had crossed the Channel only a few decades earlier, either to escape the influence of Rome or simply to carve out new realms for themselves. These were the Belgic Celts and they retained close links with their kinsmen on the European mainland. According to Caesar's account in *The Gallic War* this was the nature of the country which he found in 55 BC:

> The interior of Britain is inhabited by people who claim, on the strength of an oral tradition, to be aboriginal; the coast, by Belgic immigrants who came to plunder and make war - nearly all of them retaining the names of the tribes from which they originated - and later settled down to till the soil. The population is exceedingly large, the ground thickly studded with homesteads, closely resembling those of the Gauls, and the cattle very numerous.

One thing which neither Caesar nor Claudius found in Britain were cities, and this alone was enough to brand the inhabitants of the land as being barbarians. The Roman idea of civilisation was inextricably bound up with the practice of living in cities. Rome may have fought with or had profound disagreements with Carthage and Greece, but there was no question of dismissing the Greeks and Carthaginians as barbarians. They were city dwellers and therefore automatically, according to the mores of Rome, civilised. In Britain, as in the rest of Western Europe, the case was quite different.

Instead of cities, the Romans encountered what they described as *oppida*, (singular, *oppidum*). These were sprawling collections of huts, workshops, stables, temples and granaries, all surrounded by defensive palisades, earth banks and ditches. They were similar in many ways to hill forts, but fell far short of being considered, by even the loosest definition, cities. In Britain, Caesar stormed an *oppidum* in Hertfordshire, which was probably at Wheathamstead, and Claudius entered the *oppidum* of Camulodunum, later to become Colchester, accompanied by war elephants.

Now the *oppidum* of Camulodunum was built over and adopted by the Romans as the capital of the new province of Britannia. In other words, the Roman city of Colchester owed its existence to the large settlement which had already been there when the Romans arrived. This was not the case with Londinium, which sprang into being from nothing.

We can be confident that there was no settlement on the site of what was to become London. Caesar certainly makes no mention of anything of the sort when he describes the crossing of the Thames in 54 BC and nor do the accounts of the Claudian invasion a century or so later. To all intents and purposes, the Romans did indeed start from scratch when setting up their base on the Thames. But why choose this spot in the first place?

We saw at the beginning of the last chapter that according to *1066 and All That*, Julius Caesar: 'landed, like all other successful invaders of these islands, at Thanet'. Seaborne invasions of Britain, whether those actually undertaken by Julius Caesar, Claudius and William the Conquerer or that planned by the Nazis during the Second World War are always predicated upon a fleet of ships which keeps the coast of England in sight from embarkation until landfall. This means that such forces sail from France and arrive in England either in Kent or East Sussex. Having landed, commanders wishing to lead their troops into the heart of Britain must head north or north-west. This brings them to the Thames and they must then work their way west until they find a suitable spot to cross the river. When Caesar landed in Kent and headed inland in this way, the first point at which it was possible to cross the Thames was the ford which was roughly where Westminster Bridge stands today. Colour Plate 2 makes this a little clearer and shows why any invader landing in Kent was likely to end up crossing the Thames in London before getting to the Midlands or north of the country.

Caesar describes how his men forded the Thames during his second expedition to Britain in 54 BC and that the water came up to their necks. It is one thing to use this method of crossing a river as a one-off in the course of a military campaign, but clearly if you are going to establish a permanent presence by a strategic river crossing, you will require something a little more convenient; a bridge, for example.

During the Claudian invasion, the commanders were apparently unable to find the ford that Caesar had used and reference is made to crossing the River Thames by means of a bridge. This was presumably a pontoon bridge erected swiftly by the advancing army. It was the location of this first, temporary bridge that probably dictated the position of the camp which the Roman army established to guard this strategic river crossing. Having searched for and failed to find the ford, it is reasonable to suppose that the army was somewhere in the region of central London. The position of their first base would then be decided by the topography of the land. Obviously, it would have to be on the north bank. When the Roman soldiers crossed the Thames during the Caesar's second invasion of 54 BC, they had to endure a hail of javelins and spears from the opposite bank as they struggled across the river. Securing the north bank of the crossing place was essential.

We tend sometimes to forget that London is a city of rivers, built largely upon reclaimed marshland and swamp. When Claudius' army crossed the Thames where London would one day be built, the surrounding land would have been unrecognisable to a modern Londoner. It was a collection of islands, rivers, streams, mudflats and swamps, much of which was regularly inundated twice a day by the tidal flow of the Thames itself. Southwark was an archipelago and Westminster consisted of two or three boggy islands set in a malarial fen. There would be little point in making camp on a patch of mud that would be flooded later that day. Instead, it would be necessary to seek higher ground that was as close to the crossing point of the river as possible.

There are few hills in central London, but there are on either side of the River Thames at several points gravel terraces, covered with brick-earth. It was upon these hillocks that the city of Londinium would be built. We know these areas today as Ludgate Hill, Cornhill, Tower Hill and, on the other side of the river at Southwark, Duke Street Hill. Colour Plate 3 shows where these hills are in relation to the modern city. These would be the only logical places for the army to establish a camp which would defend their crossing point. It has been suggested that the army would have been more likely to have set up this first camp in Westminster, near the site of the ford. Hyde Park has been proposed for a possible location. There is no archaeological evidence for this, but it has been pointed out that Watling Street pointed straight to Westminster, rather than the City itself. This can easily be seen if one looks at a map and extends with a ruler the London end of Watling Street (modern-day Edgware Road). It does indeed head directly to Westminster. This has been thought by some to indicate that the roads built by the Romans originally pointed towards Westminster and not in the direction of the City of London, which is where Londinium began.

The explanation is simple and has no bearing on the location of the first Roman base in the area. Watling Street, the Roman road, followed the line of an ancient British track which certainly did cross the Thames at Westminster. That, after all, was where the ford was. Until the permanent bridge was built between Southwark and Cornhill, some time around AD 50, it is quite likely that people continued to use the ford in addition to the temporary bridge set up by the army during the invasion.

We must consider the sheer improbability of any army commander ordering his men to put up their tents in a swamp, which is what the Westminster area was at that time. Even as late as the middle ages, the land surrounding Westminster was known as Bulinga Fen, which gives a clue as to its nature. Digging ditches in such terrain would be all but impossible. In military terms too, Cornhill would be far and away the better choice for establishing an advance camp. It is dry and well drained, and unlike Westminster is on high ground and protected by rivers on two sides, the Thames to the south and Walbrook to the west. Strategically, there is no contest at all between a dry hill and a low marsh if one is looking for a defensible stronghold. There are steep slopes on the south of Ludgate Hill and Cornhill, leading down to the Thames. It is a perfect defensible position. In the late 1980s, this debate was more or less settled when the remains of a ditch from the earliest years of the invasion were uncovered at Fenchurch Street. Another section was unearthed a couple of years later and it appeared that this ditch surrounded an army camp and had been filled in soon after it was dug. It is therefore a racing certainty that there was a marching camp on Cornhill at this time. The objection has been made that such a camp could have covered an area of no more than a few acres and that perhaps there was a larger base near the Westminster ford. This may yet prove to be the case, but there is not a shred of evidence so far for the idea. At any rate, we may be confident that there was such a camp on Cornhill and that it was near this camp that the city of London sprung up over the course of the next 15 years.

To some extent, it is irrelevant where this first base was set up. The fact is that it was upon the hills of the city of London and not at Westminster, where the earliest Roman remains have been found, and it was here too that the city of Londinium was incontrovertibly built.

There has in the past been a good deal of controversy about the nature of early London. This hinges around whether or not Londinium was first established as a garrison town, as was the case with Colchester, or if it was a trading post which grew spontaneously near to the crossing point of the Thames. The current view is that it was probably a private venture, financed and built by merchants and moneylenders from abroad. The evidence for this view is not conclusive and may never be so. Briefly, the arguments for and against these two views are as follows.

In the case of Colchester, which we know was planned by the Romans to be a garrison, plenty of military artefacts have been unearthed. These are almost wholly lacking in London. The earliest sites that have been excavated, dating from around AD 50, are commercial premises rather than military buildings. On the other hand, neither are there the clusters of villas which typically surround civil municipalities and this lack is also seen around fortress towns like Colchester. The most significant point in favour of Londinium being a civil, commercial centre has already been touched upon: there are no archaeological remains of any early military architecture whatsoever, with the exception of a few indications of a temporary marching camp. There are, of course, remnants of a fort in the north-west corner of Londinium, but this was built 70 or 80 years after the invasion, long after London has become the capital of the entire province.

Whatever the nature and origins of early London, it is certain that an army camp would at first have been set up to guard the way across the Thames, particularly until the emperor himself arrived to enter Colchester in triumph and accept the submission of the British chieftains. Since this would have been the very first settlement in central London, it would be interesting to know what such a camp might have looked like. Fortunately, we already have a good deal of information about marching camps from that period. One of the divisional commanders of this campaign was Vespasian, who later became emperor himself. Twenty-five years after the Claudian invasion of Britain, when he was campaigning in the Middle East, there is a detailed, eyewitness account of one of the camps laid out by his army in time of war. There is no reason to suppose that the camp built to defend the crossing at the Thames would have been any different.

Yoseph Ben Mattithyahu was a Jew who fought against the Romans in AD 70, a leader of the revolt against Roman rule which culminated in the destruction of Jerusalem. Taken prisoner, he succeeded in ingratiating himself with his captors to the extent that he became something of a favourite of Vespasian, adopting the Romanised name of Flavius Josephus. He wrote a history of the wars between the Romans and Jews which, although politically slanted in favour of his patrons, is an excellent source for historical details. Here is Josephus' description of a temporary Roman army camp of precisely the kind that would have been set out on Cornhill in AD 43 – the earliest occupation of London known:

> A great many craftsmen accompany the army, equipped with tools, and the ground is measured and levelled if necessary, the interior of the camp is divided into rows of tents, the exterior is made like a wall with towers at regular intervals, the artillery is placed between the towers, and there are four gates wide enough for baggage animals to pass through and for the army to sally out from. There are intersecting streets, the headquarters is in the centre like a small temple, there is a workshop quarter, tribunals from which the officers can address the men, and a ditch round the outside. Once dug in, the troops take their quarters in tents by their centuries. Fatigues are performed with the same discipline and regard for security. All take their meals at the same time at signals from buglers.

This then, is what the earliest settlement in London would have been like: a camp surrounded by a defensive ditch and bank, with rows of tents like streets.

The camp described by Josephus is what is known as a marching camp. Roman soldiers could establish such a camp, it is said, in three hours. The spoil from the ditches would have been heaped up on the side of the ditch facing the camp. Wooden palisades would then surmount the bank and gates installed. Incidentally, this alone militates against the idea of such a military engineering project being conducted near Westminster. The thought of digging ditches in a swamp is frankly absurd.

Now such marching camps in Europe have been obliterated by wind and rain, leaving at best crop marks or vague indentations in the soil. There still exists a well-preserved example, though, of a Roman camp which shows us how the one in London would have looked. When the Romans were besieging the mountain fastness of Masada in Israel's Negev Desert, they built a camp at the foot of the mountain. Due to of the lack of erosion by rainfall, it is still clearly visible and may be seen in Colour Plate 4. London's first settlement would have looked just the same, with the camp filled with leather tents and drilling soldiers.

Depending upon the size of the army, such temporary bases could be extensive. Writing in the second century BC, another writer, Polybius, describes a marching camp with an area of about 88 acres. Such a camp could have been home to thousands of soldiers. When did the shift take place from temporary army camp to civilian town? We can date this pretty precisely. During excavations in the street known as Poultry, the remains of a wooden drain were found. It evidently lay in the roadway which followed the east–west line of modern-day Cheapside. This was the *Via Decumana*. There is no doubt that this was a commercial district, because the remains of shops have been found lining the street. Using dendrochronology, matching tree rings up to find the year that the wood was felled, we know that the tree from which the drain was made had been cut down in AD 47. We can therefore be confident that within four or five years of the invasion, streets had been laid out, shops built and the city of Londinium founded.

Once they had finished with a camp of this sort and were ready to move on, the army would dismantle the whole thing, burning the wooden fences, demolishing the earth banks and filling in the ditches. It would be insane to make a gift of such a stronghold to any future enemy who might chance upon it.

How did this temporary camp become transformed into the largest city of the new province, especially bearing in mind that another city entirely had already been earmarked for the capital? We start by observing that London began with an army camp, pitched upon Cornhill. The men in this camp were soldiers in a strange country. There were no shops or bars for them to visit in their off-duty hours; nothing surrounding them but grass and trees. What would such men want? They would want what any group of soldiers in a foreign country under those circumstances would: beer, girls and a bit of excitement. It cannot have been long before the first Britons started hanging around outside the gates of this camp with things to sell. Home-made beer, fresh food, dogs, ponies, jewellery, clothes, decorative weapons; practically anything which the natives might think worth exchanging. The people of south-east Britain had been trading with the Romans in this way for decades. These soldiers might have been a novelty en masse, but individual Romans were not wholly unknown. The first bartering must have taken place within days of the camp being built. Others would be offering services to the soldiers such as repairing weapons and tools.

Women would have been irresistibly drawn to the strangers' base. Then, as now, some girls would find foreign men of greatly different appearance far more attractive than the young men with whom they have grown up. A month after the Romans had first pitched their tents by the Thames, there would be the makings of a small shanty town parked as near to the army base as the commanders would tolerate: huts and lean-tos probably, stocked with beer and trinkets; perhaps a blacksmith and leatherworker or two. Quite possibly, London's first brothel would have been operating. Some of the girls who gravitated to the camp might have been interested in having a handsome and exotic boyfriend; others would have an eye to the main chance and be providing services on a strictly cash basis. This has always been the way with armies stationed abroad; it is extremely unlikely that the situation would be any different a couple of thousand years ago.

There was one other point that helped London to grow. The Thames was a political as well as a physical border. The land bordering the river on either side was a buffer zone, belonging to no tribe. This meant that London was not built in and surrounded by the territory of any one tribe. This was in sharp contrast to the situation of Colchester, which had essentially been a tribal capital before the Roman city was established there. The implications for London were profound and wholly beneficial. As it was in a no-man's-land, men and women from rival tribes could meet there in amity. They had a common purpose in coming to the Roman camp and pragmatism suggested that it was in everyone's interests to put aside old rivalries while conducting their business.

There is a minor mystery about the name of the new city. It seems likely that the name 'Londinium' was based upon some pre-existing nearby place name. Many attempts have been made to delve into the etymology of the city's name; none have been successful. It has variously been suggested that the word 'London' relates to the Celtic for 'dark river' or 'black pool', that it is based upon the Indo-European words for 'swimming' and 'river' and that its origins are even more ancient, perhaps pre-dating both the Romans and the Celts, and possibly even the Indo-Europeans. The truth is, we shall never know and such debates are accordingly pointless and sterile. The city was called Londinium, for reasons at which we can only guess. The first mention of Londinium is made by Tacitus following the Boudican revolt. He says that the city was not an official colony, but rather a place where businessmen dealt in merchandise. This, incidentally, appears to strengthen the case for those who argue against a military origin for the city.

About the river which flows through the heart of the city, we may be sure that the name of this pre-dates the foundation of London. Caesar refers to the Thames in *The Gallic War*, calling it the Tamesis. As with the name of London, we have no idea what might have been signified by the word 'Thames'. There has been much speculation about this over the years. Some have suggested that it is derived from two Celtic words, '*tam*' and '*uisghe*', *tam* meaning wide and *uisghe* meaning water, so the meaning of the name would be 'wide water'. Others believe that the name of the river is related to the Celtic words for 'dark'; the Irish word '*teimheal*' is from the same root. This would mean that the original name of the Thames simply meant something like Dark River.

The initial 'th' in Thames only dates from the sixteenth century and has never been pronounced as anything but 't'. This spelling was introduced to give a classical air to London's river; it was thought that calling it the Thames, rather than the Tames, would make it look like a Greek place name. The most we can state confidently is that the river flowing through London has for at least 2000 years been known as the Thames or *Tamesis*. It was called that before the arrival of the Romans and retained the name after they left. As with the name 'London', we are never likely to be in a position to know just what was signified by the name.

We have looked briefly at the circumstances which gave rise to the establishment of a settlement or trading centre on the banks of the River Thames. We have seen that the presence of a ford made this part of the river important and caused the Roman army to camp in the general area of London during their campaign. There is another point about the river here, which was probably unknown to the Romans when first they arrived, but which subsequently made this the ideal spot for starting a city. This is where the tidal head of the Thames is located. The river ebbs and flows with the tide and a ship travelling up the river from the North Sea would be carried along on the tide as far as London. It is also deep enough here at high tide for large ships to navigate. Until the 1970s, central London was still a sea port, with oceangoing ships unloading at the docks within sight of Tower Bridge.

A city is of course far more than the sum of its geographical features or buildings and bridges. So it was with Londinium and in the next chapter we will look at the kind of people who flocked here from across the empire in the years up to AD 60. Unlike Colchester, there was no pre-existing population; all those who came to live in this raw young city were newcomers and parvenus. This gave it the air of a frontier town, in contrast to the staid and respectable mantle it now wears after 2000 years of continuous occupation.

2

The First Londoners at Home

In this chapter we are going to look at London and the people who lived in it during its earliest years; from the invasion of AD 43 to the destruction of the whole city by Boudica's forces in AD 60. Before we look at what sort of people were living in first-century London, we are going to consider the physical nature of the place where they began building the village which was soon to become the capital of the entire province. We shall then examine the conditions under which these people lived. What would living conditions have been like for the thousands of men and relatively few women who inhabited the hills of London? To discover this, it will be necessary to rethink radically much of what we think we know about the Roman world at this time. The first point is that the size and type of structures that people erect to live and work in depends largely upon the materials which are available. If only snow is to be found nearby, then this will be used for building, as with the igloos of the Inuit. If there are a lot of mammoth bones lying around, as in prehistoric Siberia, then people will build huts from them. The same goes for wood, stone and mud.

Most of us have a mental image of what we suppose a Roman city to have looked like. This is often based upon old Hollywood films, combined with half-remembered pictures from childhood books. Typically, we see in our mind's eye gleaming white palaces and classical temples with fluted columns and triangular pediments. The rooftops are red tiled and inside these buildings the floors consist of elaborate mosaics based upon mythological themes. Fountains and frescoes finish off the scene, which is generally peopled by grave looking men in togas, strolling around while discussing philosophy and ethics. We have a tendency to impose this idealised Roman metropolis upon any city of that time of which we hear and so, for many people, this is how they imagine Londinium to have looked. The reality was very different.

To begin with, we must forget about luxurious stone-built villas. London has no ready source of stone for building. Some cities, Bath for example, have limestone quarries within spitting distance and so it was natural that when the Romans set to work there, they used this white stone as the basic building material. In London, during the first years of the Roman occupation, the natural resources available for building were earth, water, trees and grass. If one was prepared to dig down a few feet, there was also clay. It was of these basic materials that the first buildings in this area were constructed. The only noticeable differences between the style and methods of construction of these first London buildings and those already being built by the natives of southern Britain were the shape and internal division. For reasons which are obscure, the Britons lived in roundhouses, whereas the houses and shops which were going up in London were rectangular. The typical British roundhouse had no internal walls, while the buildings of this new settlement beside the Thames were divided into rooms.

When the Romans arrived in this country and their army secured the banks of the River Thames, somewhere in the area which would later become central London; what did they find? There were many marshes by the river and also a lot of small islands. The Thames was a good deal broader than it is today, now that we have constricted it between high stone embankments. Many other rivers and streams fed into the Thames here: the Fleet, the Walbrook, the Tyburn, the Neckinger and Effra. Most of these rivers vanished centuries ago and we remember them today only in the names of the streets which run above them: Fleet Street and Effra Road, for example.

There were low, grass-covered hills scattered among the fenlands which edged the river and a huge forest that stretched as far as the eye could see. These then were the resources upon which those first settlers would be compelled to rely when they began building their shops and homes along the edge of the Thames. The trees could be felled to provide timber, the earth could be scooped up and mixed with water from the rivers to make mud, and the clay and grass could be thrown into the equation as well. What sort of buildings might this produce?

We must first recall that throughout history and even today, in the twenty-first century, mud has been a valuable building material. It is free, easy to find and very versatile. When mixed with clay and dried grass or straw as well, producing what is know as cob, a building constructed of wood and mud can last for centuries. This is known as adobe in America and the remains of ancient Native American cities have been found which are made of this material. Some of these pueblos, as they are called, are several centuries old and yet look as though they might only have been abandoned yesterday.

Returning to London in the first years after the Roman invasion, how did people make use of the mud and trees which they found there? The first step would probably have been to fell trees and prepare from them beams and planks to build a framework. There is some evidence that the wooden parts of London's first buildings were prefabricated, assembled 'offsite' as builders call it. These structures were erected without any foundations. We shall see shortly what the implications of this were for those living in such a place. Once the frame was up, the walls could be fitted in place. These would typically have been panels of woven branches and twigs; the sort of thing which today we might consider a picturesque type of windbreak for the garden. Now we begin making the house habitable.

The good thing about working with mud is that there is no shortage of it and it is completely free. Readers might care to experiment themselves with this useful substance. The earth used must first be sieved to remove any large stones. It is then mixed with enough water to make something the consistency of porridge. Chopped up dry grass or straw is then added to the mix. In China it was rice husks, in Africa shredded palm, but in this country there is no shortage of grass and so that is what we shall use. As this is added to the mud, the mixture thickens and congeals. Clay can be mixed in at this stage and this will make the end product harder and more durable. Fortunately, London earth already has clay mixed in with it. At this point, one has two options; two different ways that one can use the mud for building.

Pouring the mud, clay and straw mixture into a wooden mould, or even making it a little firmer and shaping it by hand, will result in a rectangular block which can be dried in the sun. One can certainly build a fairly large structure from such bricks. A mud brick formed of London earth may be seen in Colour Plate 5. The other way to use the mud mix, and the evidence suggests that this was the most common method in early London, was to treat the semi-liquid mud as though it were plaster. It can be used to coat the woven panels of which we spoke earlier and also to seal cracks between planks. It does not look very attractive, but can later be painted. This technique is called wattle-and-daub and had been used for thousands of years. It is how the Britons were building their houses long before the Romans invaded their country. Colour Plate 6 illustrates the nature of a wattle-and-daub wall. Thin branches have been woven together and coated with a mixture of earth and clay.

A house without foundations built in this way using untreated wood and mud will have a life expectancy of around 20 to 30 years. It will last long enough for a family to raise their children to adulthood. Since life expectancy was at that time so much lower, it might well have lasted the average adult literally a lifetime. It is environmentally friendly because it will rot away to nothing after a while, leaving behind only earth, wood and decomposing straw. Britain is a damp country and rain does tend to erode a mud-covered wall. The beauty of mud, though, is that is can be repaired simply by smearing more mud over any patches which are wearing a bit thin. If you have mixed clay in with it, this erosion will not be as severe.

It is not to be supposed that buildings constructed in this way must be poky and small. Say 'mud' and the next word which comes immediately to mind is 'hut', but this reveals more about our Eurocentric prejudices than it does about the reality of building with mud. In regions where there is rather less rainfall than in London and more sun to bake mud dry, mud buildings can be can grow to immense sizes. Some of the pueblos in the southern United States are as big as towns and the world's largest mud building, the Great Mosque of Djenne in Mali, is almost 250ft long.

Nor have we exhausted the possibilities of mud as a building material. The first forts thrown up in this country by the Roman army were really just slightly more permanent versions of the marching camps at which we looked in the last chapter. They are known by archaeologists as 'turf forts'. We saw that to make mud bricks, cob or adobe, it is necessary to mix in some sort of fibrous vegetable matter. This binds the mud together and prevents it from cracking and crumbling away too readily. The Bible, of course, refers to this. When the Children of Israel were living in bondage in ancient Egypt, as related in the book of Exodus, the pharaoh of the time wished to oppress the Israelites who were making bricks for him. He commanded that they should no longer be provided with straw to make the bricks. 'Making bricks without straw' has passed into the language as a byword for an arduous or soul-destroying task. If we cut blocks of earth where grass has been growing for years, we shall not need to worry about mixing vegetable fibre in with it. It is there already in the form of a tangled root system which reaches a couple of feet into the ground.

One can build walls from turf cut into thick chunks and they will last a long while. This is because the grass roots continue to grow, binding one block to another. We can still see Bronze Age barrows, burial mounds, built from turf. Three thousand years later and they are still standing. Earth can be a very long-lasting building material; it is unlikely that any modern structure will still be standing in 3000 years' time! Houses can be made from turf as well. These were often built by pioneers in the American West and were called 'soddies'. Such houses can last for many years.

It is easy to forget that most houses in London are, even today, constructed of clay which has been dug from the ground. We are lucky in that London floats on a veritable sea of clay and so this has always been our primary building material. The bricks of which your house is made are nothing more than dried clay. There is little difference in principle between a brick-built house and an African mud hut. Both are, in effect, constructed from dried mud!

If we could be transported back to this first incarnation of London, what would it be like to live in one of these houses of which we have been talking? Excavations in recent years have uncovered an entire row of shops, in which the owners probably lived as well as carrying on their trade. We thus have a very good idea of how things were at that time. The best way to put yourself in the shoes of one of those early Londoners is to imagine that you are forced to abandon your home and move into a wooden garden shed. It is drafty and cold, not least because there is no glass in the windows. The purpose of these windows is to let light in rather than keeping the wind out. Glass is too precious to waste for keeping a house warm. At night you might have wooden shutters to provide a little insulation. Unlike a modern garden shed, there is no concrete or wooden floor, just the bare earth. Nor is there any heating or lighting. In many cases, there would be no bed either; you would have to wrap up in blankets and sleep on the ground. Try to visualise such an existence, not for a night or two as a novelty, but year after year. Think about sleeping every night on the earth in the middle of a bleak English winter and you might begin to get some idea of what life was like in London.

The average size of the rooms at the back of the shops from this period which have been excavated, where the owner and his family lived, was about 2.5m on each side; roughly the size of a small kitchen today. In one or two rooms of this size, entire families would live and work, cook and eat, sleep, make love and open their bowels. Washing facilities were, for the most part, non-existent. The floors of these homes were earth or, at best, clay. Set into a hole in one such floor has been found a large clay jar which, it is assumed, would provide the lavatory facilities for the whole family. This ties in with the practice in other cities, including Rome itself. We hear a good deal about the marvellous and up-to-date sewage disposal system in Roman times, but nothing of the sort would have benefited the ordinary worker in a provincial town like London.

With such small rooms, the corner where the family opened their bowels and voided their bladders would necessarily be only a few feet or so from the larder and hearth. When the jar was full, it would be emptied in the back yard or perhaps tipped in the nearby Walbrook stream. If the person carrying the full jar was feeling lazy, it might just be tipped out of the window or behind somebody else's house. When one considers that by AD 60 there were, according to some estimates, as many as 10,000 or 20,000 people living cheek by jowl in a 30-acre area centred around Cornhill and Southwark, the nature of the problem becomes apparent.

Quite apart from the appalling smell of all that human excrement being thrown into the street and river every day in such a restricted area, there is the matter of infection. Every well sunk in the place would have been contaminated with faeces; it would be a recipe for endemic dysentery and typhoid. There was no such thing as 'fresh water'.

The smell of unwashed bodies and excrement would have been exacerbated by the animals which many Londoners were keeping in their backyards. These walled areas at the backs of houses and shops were home to chickens and pigs. They rooted about, feeding on food scraps and adding their own contribution to the heaps of excrement thrown out of the house. The astonishing number of pupae of flies and other insects found during excavations tell us that these yards would have been swarming with flies. With no glass in the windows, so too would the interiors of the shops and homes. The presence of so many flies would hardly make the city more hygienic, nor would all the mice and other vermin attracted by the filth of the town.

The horrible smell caused by the lack of sanitation would be masked to some extent by the smoke which permeated every home. The commonest arrangement for both cooking and heating in those first years was to have a hearth in the middle of the floor of one or more of the tiny rooms. The fuel for such fires was provided by wood and dried animal dung. During the winter, it would be necessary to keep a fire going for 24 hours a day. At night, people would wrap up warmly and sleep on the floor around the fire. There are a number of serious disadvantages to this way of life.

The most obvious hazard of living in a small room with an open fire blazing in the middle of the floor is the chance of somebody tripping and falling into the fire, or rolling over and finding one's clothes smouldering during the night. This would be a particular hazard if there were children about. The risk of accidental fires must have been tremendous. Imagine lighting an open fire inside a wooden garden shed today; how often could one do this regularly without burning the thing down? There is abundant archaeological evidence that fires of this sort were frequent.

Another question to consider is that of lighting. We most of us have some vague idea about lamps fuelled by olive oil being used in Roman times. Well this is true as far as it goes, but we must bear two points in mind. First, lamps burning olive oil might be relatively bright, compared perhaps with a stick of burning wood, but by today's standards they would still be pretty feeble. Such a lamp would typically provide less light than a modern candle, but would have to illuminate an entire room for hours at a time. The second consideration is that for most of those living in Londinium at that time, even a lamp of this sort would be an unaffordable luxury. A lot of people would not have the money for the imported olive oil needed to run a lamp. For them, rush-lights would be the main source of light at night. These consisted of a dry reed which had been dipped in animal fat repeatedly until it was as thick as a slender candle. They produce smelly, sooty, greasy smoke as a byproduct. As an easy experiment in practical archaeology, I urge readers to dip a piece of string in heated animal fat, let it dry and then repeat the process a few times until something resembling a candle has been produced. Then light the end of the string. Only by doing this will it be possible to understand what a mess such lighting makes.

These houses did not have chimneys and so all the smoke, soot, fumes and cooking smells would have filled the cramped room continuously. The constant breathing in of wood smoke and soot in an enclosed space is yet another of those things which would have a deleterious effect upon the health of those living under such conditions for years at a time.

One final point which we must consider is that most of these homes would lack even the most basic furniture such as tables, beds and chairs. Even in Rome itself, at the height of its prosperity, ordinary citizens often made do without anything other than a sleeping mat, one set of clothes and a wooden bowl. If one is sleeping round an open fire most nights, then a bed will be useless; one wishes to be right by the embers. And why would one need a cupboard if one had no clothes or other belongings to store in such a thing? It would be a pointless luxury. The poet Martial said that in

Rome a poor man had a toga, a mattress, a rush mat and a cup. The situation was much the same in London, at least in the first decade or two of its existence. Quite apart from any other consideration, the rooms of those early homes were so cramped that there simply would not have been room for any furniture. People sat, ate and slept on the bare earth floor of their tiny rooms.

Having gained some idea of the domestic life of the average citizen living in London before AD 60, we shall now venture into the streets of the city and look at the broader picture. Before doing so, let us sum up the situation of the average person living in London at this time. His lifestyle would be roughly comparable to that of a peasant living in one of the more impoverished villages in present-day Bangladesh. Clean water would be an unattainable dream; he would live in cramped and insanitary conditions, sleeping on the bare earth. His home would be dirty and smoky and his life expectancy at birth would be 25 years. Life expectancy in modern Bangladesh, a very poor country, is 69.

We have already touched upon some of the reasons for this appallingly low life expectancy. Sleeping on bare earth in damp, draughty conditions will not do anybody much good in the long run, especially in the winter. The constant breathing in of smoke and soot will not help matters either. One must suppose that respiratory disorders were endemic in Roman London. Having no source of water to wash one's hands before handling food would also be a recipe for ill health, as would having the lavatory facilities within a few feet of the larder and cooking fire. The water drawn from wells and streams for drinking and cooking would in all probability be heavily contaminated with human waste. The constant dumping of the contents of chamber pots in back yards and alleyways would ensure that any infectious disease suffered by one person would rapidly spread to his neighbours. Many people would suffer from worms. This would be more than an inconvenience.

Tape worms can spread from the intestines to other parts of the body, including the lungs, muscles and brain. Once there, they form cysts which can be life threatening. The usual mode of transmission of these parasites from one person to another is via water contaminated with human faeces. As we have seen, such water was all that was available to the early Londoners and such infestations must accordingly have been endemic.

What would this city look and sound like? Most of us subconsciously think of Roman cities as being calm and dignified places. Even in Rome itself, let alone a newly built port town like London, this was not true. Martial, who lived in Rome during the first century AD, was very clear about how noisy and chaotic the city was. He wrote:

> On one side of the street there's the moneychanger idly rattling his coppers on a dirty table, while on the other side the goldsmith's beating gold plate with his mallet. There's an incessant stream of soldiers, shipwrecked sailors with their bodies swathed in bandages, Jewish beggars and salesmen selling sulphur.

Elsewhere, he complains that: 'There's nowhere a poor man can get any quiet in Rome. The laughter of the passing throng wakes me and Rome is at my bed's head.' Seneca too writes of the awful noise in Rome and it is one of the features of the city most complained about by classical writers.

The entire city was a hubbub of shopkeepers calling out the virtues of their wares, soldiers shouting and cursing, workman hammering and sawing, animals bleating and neighing. This racket continued day and night. After dark, bakers would still be at work in their kitchens, the taverns would be full and drunken people would sing and shout. This is not the Rome with which we are familiar at all.

If the venerable city of Rome, which had been established centuries earlier, was so noisy, what on earth would the 30-acre site of London have been like at that time? The population was growing exponentially at this time. From nobody at all in AD 43, the number of people crowded on to the hills of Cornhill, Ludgate and Southwark had grown in 13 years to somewhere in the region of 10,000 or 20,000. This means that apart from visitors coming and going, the permanent population of London was increasing by 15 to 30 every week for years on end. All those extra people would have needed somewhere to live, which argues for the place resembling one large building site, with workmen shouting and banging about all day.

Think also that this was a port and that because of the small size of the place, one would never be more than a couple of hundred yards or so from the docks. Every day, ships would be docking and unloading, with all the attendant noise. Although the army had in the main moved to other parts of the country, units on route from Europe would have to pass through London on their way to the frontier.

What would the city have looked like at this time? It would have presented a drab enough appearance; this was a working environment, not a tourist attraction. During excavations of buildings which were destroyed by fire in AD 60, one was found to have been coated with plaster which had been painted white. This was the exception; in the main these would have been wooden-framed, single storey-buildings, the walls woven from twigs and covered with clay. Some would be built from planks. Perhaps one or two would be painted; the rest would be in various shades of dull brown, the natural colours of wood and sun-dried clay. Why were these building so cramped and poky? After all, there was plenty of room for building; no worries about encroaching on a green belt. It is purely physical limitation. Putting together a one-storey building the size of a garden shed is fairly simple. One can throw up such a structure in a few days. Making the walls strong enough to withstand a wind is one thing; making them sufficiently sturdy to support a second storey is another entirely. This was a hastily built settlement where speed in building was of the essence. None of the houses and shops which have been excavated from this time have any proper foundations; they were erected by driving posts directly into the earth. This too contributed to the cramped and crowded feel of the place, because some of these buildings would be leaning against each other like rows of terraced houses.

The main street of London was the *Via Decumena*, which ran east to west from one hilltop to another. It straddled Cornhill and Ludgate Hill, crossing the Walbrook River a few yards west of the Bank of England. Once again, we must confront the dramatic difference between a little frontier town of this sort and the amenities in a large city like Rome. We have all heard of the great sewer which flowed beneath the streets of ancient Rome. The *Cloaca Maxima* was so wide that it was said a wagon loaded with hay could be driven along it. The equivalent in London at this time was a wooden gulley which ran along the centre of the mud track which was the *Via Decumena*. A tributary of the Walbrook had been diverted into this drain, which discharged into the Walbrook itself. Both the drain and the Walbrook were open sewers, into which people threw all kinds of filth of which they wished to dispose, including the contents of their chamber pots.

These days, anybody with a patch of land in London will build upwards. Land is expensive and we have the technology to construct soaring towers. If shops or pubs have living quarters attached to them, these will be above the premises, rather than behind. Because of the limitations of building with wattle-and-daub and no foundations, shops and business premises in

Roman London tended to have the living quarters behind the shop. This made for very narrow, single-storey properties with the thin end facing on to the street. In Colour Plate 7, we see a plan of part of the *Via Decumena*, based upon what we have discovered through excavations. Some of these shops would be leaning against each other; others might be separated from their neighbours by narrows alleys covered in gravel. This arrangement was typical of both Italian and Gaulish towns at this time and indicates that many Londoners came from these two countries. Each building has several open hearths and one can see that once a fire began, it would be very diffi-cult to contain it. On the edge of town were traditional British roundhouses of the sort to be seen all across the country. At the back are enclosed yards which serve as both middens and a place to keep poultry and livestock.

What sort of people would have been living in these miserable conditions and why? We have surmised it likely that the first permanent inhabitants of central London would have been legionaries living in tents, enclosed by the banks and ditches of a Roman marching camp. They would have been based near to the crossing point of the Thames and their role would be to guard this crossing and secure it from any enemies. The archaeological evi-dence may be scant, but human nature has not changed all that much over the last couple of millennia. It should accordingly be fairly simple to work out who was living in Londinium in its earliest years.

What we have described so far is the kind of spontaneous settlement which tended to grow up next to Roman forts in this country. This first, haphazard collection of rickety shops, blacksmiths, carpenters and so on would not have amounted to much, if this was to be the full extent of set-tlement on the hills of London. For these huts to become the capital of the province required something more. Left to themselves, the Britons might have developed the district into a sort of miniature *oppidum* or large village; what actually happened was that a Roman city emerged here. To under-stand how this happened, we must consider one of the pressures at which we looked in Chapter 1: the incentive to expand the empire beyond the Mediterranean seaboard for commercial reasons.

Producers of goods and the merchants and traders who sell on those goods are always looking for new markets. After all, the more people who are buying your wine or pottery, the more money you will make. Running your business in competition with dozens or even hundreds of other similar businesses means that the market dictates what prices you may charge and what sort of mark-ups are acceptable. What every manufacturer dreams of is cornering the market and holding a monopoly upon some product. This is all but impossible in a country full of similar operations, but if one can only find virgin territory with no competitors and thousands of customers who have no idea of the going rate for what you are selling ...

Britain had proved profitable in a small way for Roman traders for many years. There were risks in such business though; the same hazards that European traders found in nineteenth-century Africa and American entrepreneurs encountered when selling goods to the Native Americans. The natives may well take a liking to your stocks of wine or whisky, guns or Samian ware pottery. What happens though if you find yourself surrounded by a bunch of surly and hostile natives and instead of bargaining for what you have to sell, they simply cut your throat and make off with all your wares without it costing them a penny? This would not happen if there were a military presence nearby to protect your interests. You could set up shop in the shadow of a military base and this would provide you with a little security. Something of the sort must surely have been going through the minds of the merchants and businessmen who had been pressing the Roman Republic to expand the limits of Roman territory in all directions. Only the security of knowing that their army had subjugated the place would make Britain a magnet for trade. Until then, the game was just too risky for most people.

One imagines that as soon as news of Claudius' great triumph in Britain reached the ears of some of the merchants and traders back in Rome, they said to their wives in Latin, 'Come on darling, pack your bags; there's a fortune to be had just for the asking'. Some evidence to support this version of events is found in the writings of Tacitus. Since his father-in-law was Agricola, one-time governor of Britain, it is generally assumed that he had access to official papers when writing his histories of Britain and Germany. Tacitus described Londinium by saying that it 'did not rank as a Roman settlement, but was an important centre for businessmen and merchandise'.

There are two significant points about this short sentence. First, London 'did not rank as a Roman settlement'. This is an extraordinary statement to make about the town which would within a few years become the recognised capital of the whole province. What can Tacitus have meant by it? He intended to convey that Londinium, unlike say Colchester, was not a colony. At Colchester, discharged soldiers were given land and became the first inhabitants of a new town. This gave the city the status of a *colonia* or colony. This evidently did not happen in Londinium.

The second intriguing point about Tacitus' description of the city is the word he uses for 'businessmen'. He uses a Latin word which signifies those handling money and finance, rather than merchants or shopkeepers. From its very founding, right up to today, it seems that the city of London has been the centre of financial affairs in this country. These newcomers were apparently bankers, financiers and money lenders, as well as traders and shopkeepers.

Now the provincial capital was to be in Colchester. For some reason, the private interests that were investing in the new province decided to ignore this town and focus instead upon Londinium. That this should be the case requires a little explanation. Colour Plate 8 shows a map of the roads of Roman Britain. It is immediately apparent that they converge not on Colchester, but upon London. This makes perfect sense, because those landing in Kent and wishing to travel overland to the rest of the country will, as we explained in the last chapter, have had to go via London. London is more central and makes a far more convenient starting point for travelling to the rest of the country than Colchester, which is a little out of the way. This was not an artefact of the Romans, but rather a pre-existing situation. The famous Roman roads often followed the line of British tracks which were already in use; Watling Street is a good example of this. This fits in with another feature of London which makes it of great interest commercially: it is on a tidal river which is deep enough for oceangoing vessels to negotiate their way right into the heart of the city. Goods landed in Essex or Kent would have to be transported overland, passing through London anyway en route to their final destination in other parts of the country. By shipping them straight to London, a large part of this awkward journey could be avoided.

Making Colchester the provincial capital was not part of a carefully considered plan. It was the site of an *oppidum* and building a Roman town there would make a very clear statement to the natives about who exactly was in charge now. In the end, private enterprise proved to have a shrewder sense of the best location for a new capital. Claudius may have had his moment of triumph, entering the *oppidum* at Colchester with his elephants, but it was the merchants and money lenders, investing their own wealth in the newly established province that correctly identified the right place for the capital. This was demonstrated a couple of decades later, when Londinium was recognised as the de facto capital of the province and Colchester faded into insignificance. One might call it market forces in operation. The Roman leadership had, in effect, attempted to 'rig the market' by making an arbitrary choice for the leading city of the new territory. People voted with their money and feet, though, deciding that Londinium was a far better bet.

Just to recap, a Roman marching camp is set up on the banks of the Thames. Local people are drawn to it for various reasons, mainly to do with making money. It lies on a strategic crossroads, where a bridge meets several important routes to various parts of the country. Traders and businessmen from across the empire make a beeline for the area. They are intent on exploiting the new province economically. These are the spivs and wide boys, the chancers and adventurers. Some are looking to make a quick buck by ripping off the ignorant natives, while others are going to make money by lending money out at interest to the Romans living here. Others target the British tribal leaders and lend them large sums of money as well; a practice which was to have disastrous consequences for the embryonic city. There are those hoping to make a fortune by buying things from the Britons at cut price; anything from pearls to dogs, gold to slaves. Also in the rush are men planning to sell things to the tribesman of Britain: pottery, olives, wine, statues, whatever will turn a quick profit. Essentially, these are all 'get rich quick' merchants who have turned up hoping to make a swift fortune.

We have no idea how many of these newcomers would have been Romans and how many Gauls, Greeks or other nationalities. The archaeological evidence suggests strongly that there were many cultural influences at work in Londinium apart from that of the Romans themselves.

The money lenders who landed in Londinium around AD 47 would not have been the sort of men to build their own houses. They would expect others to do it for them. Those in turn who were building the house would not have been the same men who chopped down the trees which would provide the framework for the house. Nor would they be the same men who dug up the clay to line the walls. Another group would be the labourers who dug the ditch in which the first drains were laid. All sorts of people would be needed to maintain the lifestyle which some of these newcomers would expect to live. Cooks, cleaners, labourers, washerwomen, gardeners, grooms, seamstresses, hairdressers, barbers; the list is extensive. Some of those arriving in the new city would bring their own servants with them, slaves, but there would still be plenty of casual work for those prepared to up sticks from the countryside and move in with the occupiers.

The temporary army camps would within a short time have moved on. The conquest of the new province did not happen overnight. The south-east might have succumbed swiftly to the invaders, but they were to encounter fierce opposition in other parts of the country. What was in effect the front line was moving north and west, towards northern Britain and Wales. Londinium was on its own now. It had not been set up by the leadership in Rome and would now have to sink or swim by its own efforts.

Some of the speculators and carpet baggers who fetched up in Londinium would be organisers; men with the money and influence to dictate that shops would be built here, a residential street there. From the very beginning, the city has the appearance of some species of planning. It may have grown organically from the group of Britons who first began hanging round the army camp, but it did not grow in a random or haphazard way. Some group of men was deciding on the general layout. We begin to see where the old people and those attached to the place came from; those whom Tacitus says did not flee when Boudica attacked from the north. Men found work and lodgings in the town and then discovered that there was also work available for their widowed mothers or elderly aunts; as cleaners or cooks perhaps. They would send for these relatives and allow them to live with them. The standard of living for these itinerant workers would be better than that in their villages and farms; there would be a steady stream of Britons looking for work in the new port.

This was a frontier town. Jetties were being thrown up to unload the ships which were now arriving; buildings were springing up like mushrooms; the air was full of the sound of hammering and sawing. A vibrant, bustling, raw, young port town. Some estimates suggest that by the time of Boudica's uprising Londinium had as many as 20,000 citizens. If this is anything like the true figure, it is astounding. It means that over those 13 years of which we spoke earlier, 30 new, permanent residents must have been coming to Londinium every single week.

Not all these new Londoners would have been shopkeepers or bankers. One wonders what drew those who were not intending to set up shops or money lending operations in the new town. One can quite see that people would come to visit Londinium in order to buy imported goods and so on, but what was luring those 30 people a week who were coming here to live? One feels instinctively that a Wild West-type town like this would have attracted young or at the most middle-aged men. This was a thriving new port, a noisy place of opportunity, not a place to retire. It had no history at all and none of those living and working there had been born in Londinium.

We have looked closely at the city of London as it was in the first 15 years or so after its founding. We have examined the type of buildings to be found there and also seen what sort of people would be living in those buildings. Early London was a bustling port, a roistering and lively, raw, young town, full of men on the make who had come from all over Europe and the Middle East. There was only one thing missing in the new city which had sprung up on the banks of the Thames. We all have 20/20 hindsight and in retrospect it is so very easy to see what those first Londoners left out of their calculations. They assumed that the only things they needed to worry about were taxes and tariffs, imports and exports, finding an angle and offering a better rate than the trader or money lender in the next street. After all, this was a city of businessmen, not an army town.

The one fatal error made by those who caused the city to grow by their industry in those first years after the invasion was defence. But then, why should this have occurred to them? It was 17 years since Claudius' legions had seized and occupied this country. There was still fighting, but the front line was hundreds of miles away in Wales and the northern parts of the country up towards Scotland. The rest of the province had been pacified and was well on the way to being as civilised as the rest of the Roman world. Why on earth would those living in London need any defences? The city lay open to the world until AD 60. It was then, with the Roman forces off campaigning in North Wales, that the need for some kind of defensive architecture became apparent to the inhabitants of the city.

3

Destruction and Rebirth

The details of the uprising led by Queen Boudica against the occupying forces of the Roman army are too well known to need recounting in detail here. Briefly, Boudica was the wife of the King of the Iceni tribe in Norfolk. When her husband, who was supposedly an ally of Rome, died he left half his kingdom to his daughters and the rest to the Emperor of Rome. The Romans came up with a much better idea. They ignored his will and, treating the territory as if it had been conquered by force of arms, they seized it all. When his widow objected they had her flogged, while at the same time raping her daughters. This was, of course, bad enough, but there were other causes for complaint both among the tribes of East Anglia and across the whole of Britain. Many of the native inhabitants of Colchester had been evicted from their land to make way for the building of a Roman town and a huge, classical temple for the worship of the deified emperor Claudius had been raised in the new town. To add insult to injury, this offensive symbol of colonial oppression had been paid for by taxation of those who had lost their homes. They were being forced to finance an ostentatious and vulgar structure, the purpose of which was for people to worship as a god the man who had enslaved them and deprived them of their land. Little wonder that this should have caused unrest as, any other consideration not withstanding, this temple for the worship of an ordinary man offended deeply against the religious sensibilities of the native Britons. This tied in with another grievance; one which was not limited to the Iceni and neighbouring tribes.

Another reason that the country in general had for becoming restive was that a large part of the Roman army of occupation had gone north to Wales in order to destroy the Druid stronghold on the island of Anglesey. The Druids had been a thorn in the flesh of the Romans since the conquest of Gaul a century earlier. They were an educated elite who served as a nexus of subversion and discontent in the Celtic lands. Their influence was political as well as religious and they acted as advisors and counsellors to the tribal chiefs. Britain was the centre of Druid power in the whole of Europe and Anglesey was their holiest sanctuary. The Romans had decided to break the power of the Druid priesthood once and for all. This military operation was pivotal in the development of the Boudican uprising, providing both motive and opportunity. The concerted attack on their ancestral religion provided the motive, while the absence of so much of the army from the rest of Britain gave the opportunity for Britons in the south-east to launch an assault on the occupiers of their land.

There was a third cause of the uprising which took place in south-east Britain at that time, but we will examine this in Chapter 6, since it is more properly a matter of commerce than of political or military affairs. It is enough for now to consider that the mistreatment of a noble woman was probably not enough in itself to trigger the insurgency and that even the attack on the headquarters of their ancestral religion might not have been sufficient provocation to start a war. Most wars then, as now, when stripped of the fancy rhetoric and appeals to elevated sentiments and high-minded principles, are really nothing more than money squabbles. It is quite possible that this was also the case with the Boudican revolt.

Boudica was regarded by the Romans as a terrifying figure. An historian described her physical appearance as 'huge of frame, terrifying of aspect, and with a harsh voice. A great mass of bright red hair fell to her knees: she wore a twisted torc, and a tunic of many colours, over which was a thick mantle, fastened by a brooch.'

The Romans did not treat women as equals and probably felt that their treatment of the Iceni queen and her daughters would be enough to put them in their place. Celtic women, though, were in many ways at least the equal of their menfolk. Just because the Romans held their women to be of little account politically or socially did not mean that other nations necessarily followed the same ideas. Having whipped this troublesome woman and abused her daughters, they felt that they could now dismiss her from their minds. This was perhaps the gravest mistake the Romans made during their 400-year occupation of this island.

Following her humiliation at the hands of the Romans, Boudica gathered tens of thousands of warriors to her cause and swept south to Colchester. Other tribes besides the Iceni soon joined the revolt. It began to seem possible to them that here was a chance to throw off the Roman yoke. After all, the invaders had at this point only been in the country for a mere 17 years; a short enough time for it to appear to the British that this military occupation might be a temporary matter which could be swept away with sufficient determination and courage on the part of the rightful owners of the land. Although it had been originally established as a fortified, military base, after 17 years of peaceful life Colchester was now an open town. There had been earth walls, but these had been deliberately levelled; they had obstructed the town's expansion. The city accordingly had no defences and was populated largely by retired old soldiers who had been rewarded for their long army service by being given grants of land. These colonists sent urgent appeals for help to the procurator in London. The procurator, essentially the financial manager of the province, sent all the troops he could muster, which amounted to just 200 lightly armed auxiliaries. The scale of the rebellion was not yet apparent to those in the rest of the country, otherwise it would have been obvious that a couple of hundred men could make not the slightest difference to the eventual outcome of the battle when faced by a force of 50,000 or 60,000 armed men.

Colchester was besieged. After a couple of days' stand-off, Boudica and her supporters overran the place, killing everybody they found living there, Roman and Briton alike. The last of the defenders took refuge with their families in the great temple of Claudius. The significance of this must have delighted the fierce warriors who surrounded this hated emblem of colonial power. They were already incensed that a foreign army had gone to Wales, seeking to wipe out the holy sanctuary of their own religion. Now the terrified compatriots of these men were holed up in the very temple which was itself an affront to the religious and cultural sensibilities of every right-thinking Briton. They must have clashed their swords and spears against their shields and shouted with joy. As we would say today, this was time for payback. One can hardly be surprised that they torched the temple, making a burnt offering to their gods of the sacrilegious wretches sheltering within. There were no survivors.

We do not know how word reached the military governor in Wales of the growing insurgency. What we do know is that messages were sent to military bases in south-east Britain, asking them to dispatch troops to the defence of Colchester. The Ninth Legion was given orders to march on the city to deal firmly with the rebels. They were stationed near Peterborough in Cambridgeshire and marched from there towards Colchester. This would be a route march of some 75 miles and even tough Roman soldiers could be expected to take three days to cover this distance. It is unlikely that the entire legion was involved in this action. More probable is that there were around 2000 infantry, accompanied by perhaps 500 cavalry.

Somewhere near Colchester, the Ninth Legion was ambushed by Boudica's men. According to Tacitus, the infantry were massacred to a man and only the cavalry were able to escape. It was a crushing blow for the Romans, their worst military defeat in Britain. Flushed now with their success and feeling themselves to be invincible, the Britons spent some time looting the remains of Colchester and revelling in their victory. They then headed south-west. Their next target was London.

London symbolised all that the British tribes living their traditional lives loathed about the Romans and those who collaborated with them. They were dainty and effete, eating unfamiliar foods which had to be brought here from other countries. British beer was not good enough for them; they only drank wine. They dressed differently and were arrogant and rude to the people whose country they had occupied. All this was a bad enough way for the Romans and other foreigners to carry on, but special hatred was reserved for those Britons who had chosen to ape their masters and adopt their style of living. Such people were the worst sort of traitors to their own country and could expect no mercy from Boudica's men. Quislings and fifth columnists have never been very popular at the best of times and London was full of them.

It is customary to describe the vast mob who headed towards London in the late summer of AD 60 as being an army, but this was not really the case at all. We know, from the descriptions of the final battle between the insurgents and the regular army ranged against them, that the British had brought their families with them on this crusade. They were defeated in the end partly because they had parked their wagons and carts near to the battlefield, so that their wives and children could have a good view of the action. On leaving the smoking ruins of Colchester, Boudica and her followers were accompanied by their relatives and children; there can hardly have been a stranger 'army' in the history of Britain. Some classical sources claim that over 200,000 people were involved, but that is certainly a ludicrous exaggeration. The historian who quoted this figure lived 150 years after the events he described. It is unlikely that a third of this number were actually heading for London at the end of the summer. Even so, a heavily armed mob 60,000 or 70,000 strong would still be a formidable force to be reckoned with.

Boudica and her people did not hurry. Theirs was not a forced route march, but a leisurely stroll, with plenty of time to stop off en route at isolated Roman villas and farms, slaughtering the occupants and helping themselves to provisions. Hundreds, perhaps thousands of chariots led the way, followed by the mass of people on foot. Horse and carts followed at the rear – the baggage train of this incredible and apparently unstoppable force. They visited the settlement of Chelmsford and burnt it to the ground after the ritual massacre and looting. We do not know how long they took to travel the 55 miles or so from Colchester to London, but it was probably weeks. Time at least for those in London to dispatch messages to the army in Wales, alerting them to the scale of the calamity that was about to befall the province.

By the time that Suetonius Paulinus, the governor of Britain, received the messages from London warning him of the impending catastrophe, he and his army had razed the Druids' sanctuary at Anglesey to the ground and killed everybody upon whom they could lay their hands. The governor, who was also the military commander of the entire province, raced to London with his cavalry arriving there a few days before Boudica. He took stock of the situation and came to a cold-blooded decision, shockingly callous but strategically quite correct. He could not hope to hold this city with no defences of any sort against an army tens of thousands strong. He was faced with the appalling choice of making a doomed last stand in London, fighting to the death and eventually succumbing to the overwhelming forces ranged against him, or retreating at once and regrouping elsewhere, hoping to fight a battle at a time and place of his own choosing. He chose this latter option.

As we saw at the end of the last chapter, because London was founded as a commercial venture by businessmen and traders, rather than as a garrison town by the army, no attempt had been made to fortify the town. It is possible that its boundaries had been delineated by a shallow ditch, or something of that kind, but there were certainly no walls or defensive earthworks. The city stood wide open.

We come now to a slight mystery. When Boudica and her army threatened London after they had destroyed Colchester, the military commander made the perfectly correct but still somewhat disconcerting decision to abandon the city and preserve his troops for a battle which they had a chance of winning. Writing of this, Tacitus, whom we may remember has access to the official records of Britain at this time, said the following. He wrote that the retreating army allowed those capable of keeping up with them to join the column. Referring to Suetonius Paulinus, he said:

> At first, he hesitated whether to stand and fight there. Eventually, his numerical inferiority … decided him to sacrifice the single city of Londoninium

to save the province as a whole. Unmoved by the lamentations and appeals, Suetonius gave the signal for departure. The inhabitants were allowed to accompany him. But those who stayed because they were women or old, or attached to the place, were slaughtered by the enemy.

This really is a most surprising statement. Where did these old people come from? How could anybody feel so attached to a new town which had not existed more than a dozen years ago, so fond of it that they would rather stay and face the wrath of Boudica instead of fleeing for their lives? Nobody living in London could have been under any illusions about the fate awaiting them when the Queen of the Iceni hit town. Yet there were some who were too old to escape or too fond of London to make the attempt. Both common sense and archaeological evidence indicate that most of the people in London in AD 60 would be men. Tacitus, though, talks of women who were unable to keep up with the army during their retreat. It would be interesting to know whether these women, old people and those attached to the place were Roman colonists or British collaborators. Perhaps, as was suggested earlier, they were the relatives of Britons who had managed to find well-paid jobs in the new town. As we shall see below, though, it seems possible that some at least were Roman women and what they were doing in this rough new port is not at all clear, unless they were the daughters and wives of businessmen.

The Roman commander assembled his forces and prepared to march out, leaving London and its citizens to their fate. He probably headed north, back along Watling Street in the direction from which he had come. His cavalry had outpaced the infantry units, who were presumably waiting for their commander somewhere in the Midlands. Those who were physically fit and prepared to abandon all they owned marched with the army. Other refugees must have crowded into the ships at harbour, hoping to flee in that way, as the procurator had already done. Others might perhaps have trekked south or made their way towards Canterbury or the other Roman-occupied towns of Kent. And some people, for whatever reason, stayed. Surely everybody must have had some idea as to what Boudica's plans were for the city. It is, of course, possible that they clung to the faint hope that Boudica would bypass London altogether and head instead to St Albans.

When the insurgents arrived, they wasted no time in trying to distinguish between Roman and Briton, male or female, young or old; they slaughtered everybody they found. The descriptions of what actually befell these people are still shocking 2000 years later. Tacitus tells us that 'there was no form of savage cruelty from which the angry victors refrained'. Elsewhere, he explains that the Britons never took prisoners, either to sell as slaves or to exchange for their own people who might have been captured. Their rule was 'no quarter to be asked nor given'. Considering the nature of the enemy against whom they were fighting, this is not really surprising. The Romans were not noted in antiquity for their gentleness and mercy towards those whom they had defeated in battle. Little wonder then that once they had the upper hand, the British, as Tacitus observes, 'could not wait to cut throats, hang, burn and crucify'.

The historian Dio, writing some years after the event, helpfully explained in greater detail what happened, particularly to the women who had stayed in London:

> Those who were taken captive by the Britons were subjected to every known outrage. The worst and most bestial atrocity committed by their captors was as follows. They hung up naked the noblest and most distinguished women and then cut off their breasts and sewed them to their mouths, in order to make the victims appear to be eating them; afterwards they impaled the women on sharp skewers run lengthways through the entire body.

Two things strike one immediately about this account. First, the symbolism of impaling the women with sharp skewers was clearly a savage revenge devised by Boudica for the rape of her daughters. It was a fiendishly ingenious way of getting her own back upon the Romans. The second thing which springs to mind is that Dio would hardly refer to British women as being either 'noble' or 'distinguished'. It is pretty plain that there were Roman women living in London, women who had for whatever reason been abandoned to their fate.

There is some evidence which indicates the ultimate fate of those caught in the city. For many years, decapitated heads have turned up during excavations in London. Many have been found in the bed of the Walbrook River, which flowed through the heart of pre-Boudican London. No other bones have been found associated with these skulls, just the heads by themselves. It has been suggested that the Celts, who were of course enthusiastic headhunters, chopped off the heads of their prisoners when they had finished torturing them and lobbed them in the river. The Thames too has yielded quite a few skulls. Once again, it is only the skulls which surface; no other parts of the skeleton. This would seem to rule out one theory for the presence of these heads in the archaeological record, the idea that they have simply been washed into rivers by heavy rainfall or floods in cemeteries. If this were the case, then we should expect to find a whole jumble of human bones, not just one particular kind.

Geoffrey of Monmouth, the medieval historian who gave us the tale of King Arthur and the Knights of the Round Table, tells a curious story about the Walbrook, which he calls the Gallebrok. He says that in ancient times many Romans were beheaded near this stream and their heads thrown in it. It is by no means impossible that we have here an authentic, albeit distorted, folk memory of the events of AD 60. The Celts were very fond of water from a religious viewpoint and many rivers, streams and wells were thought to have minor gods and goddesses dwelling in them. Offering them the heads of conquered enemies would be exactly the sort of thing one would expect. A bronze head of Claudius, wrenched from a statue of him that stood in Colchester, was found in a stream in Suffolk some years ago. It had lain their since the Boudican revolt. This was a symbolic decapitation of an enemy and it is perhaps significant that this trophy as well was ultimately cast into a river.

Archaeologists owe Boudica something of a debt of gratitude when they are trying to work out the geographical extent of Roman London in the years before AD 60. When the British had finished massacring the inhabitants of the city in various disgusting ways, they looted the place and then set fire to it. Since the buildings were all of wood and many had thatched roofs, the whole city went up like a tinderbox. We saw in the last chapter that clay was used extensively in the building of London. It was smeared on to panels of woven twigs in the style of construction known as wattle-and-daub and the floors of many homes also had floors of bare earth which contained a high proportion of London clay.

Clay is often a pale and sickly colour until it has been fired. It then becomes rich red or brown, ranging from shades of terracotta all the way through to an almost ruby red. When Boudica's people torched the city, as they had done Colchester, it burned it to the ground. The heat generated by this fire was extraordinary. Tests on some burnt pottery tell us the temperature was over 1000°C. This is comparable with the temperature generated by the firestorm which Allied bombing produced in Hamburg during the Second World War. Heat of this intensity is enough to melt some metals and alloys, including bronze, silver and gold. It is more than sufficient to cause the chemical changes in clay which we call 'firing'.

If one digs down 13ft below the present-day street level, one comes to the so-called 'red layer'. This is a stratum of fired clay about 18in thick. It is pretty well all that remains of the first city of London. The red layer is nothing other than the clay covering the walls and floors of houses burnt by Boudica. This red layer helps us to work out the extent of pre-Boudican London. For instance, until a few years ago, it was thought that Southwark was settled later than the north bank of the Thames. It now seems that this was not the case. During an excavation, the distinctive red layer was uncovered in Southwark as well, showing that Boudica and her followers found enough buildings south of the river to be worth setting fire to. This 'red layer' is also known, for obvious reasons, as the 'Boudican Destruction Horizon'.

It is likely that London's bridge was also destroyed at the same time as the fledgling city. It would have been mad to leave it intact, thus providing a handy crossing point for Roman troops coming from Kent. There is, of course, no 'red layer' under water, but the logic of burning the bridge linking the two parts of London is inescapable.

When Boudica moved north towards St Albans, she left behind a smouldering ruin. Acres and acres of charred wood and fired clay would be all that remained when the refugees returned, following the defeat of Boudica somewhere in the west Midlands. It must have been a disheartening sight indeed: 30 acres of smoking ruin, with not a single building left standing. Strangely, this disaster was to mark not the end of London, but its beginning. The destruction of Colchester, London and St Albans provided the impetus for a massive rethinking of the best location for the capital of the province of Britain. Already, before its destruction, the procurator had been based there; it made sense for the military governor too to be in London. All roads might lead to Rome in Europe, but in Britain, all roads led to London. A glance at Colour Plate 8 illustrates this point perfectly. London lay at the centre of a spider's web of important roads. Colchester, by comparison, is very much off the beaten track and not on the way to anywhere in particular.

London's rebirth was swift. The first incarnation of the city may have grown haphazardly on this spot, but its founding now was a deliberate decision by the authorities. Once the flames of Boudica's revolt had died down and the customary vengeance visited upon those who had dared to challenge Rome, a cool and calculated choice was made to abandon Colchester as the nominal capital of the province and instead to focus attention upon London.

The main outline of the streets would still have been visible, despite the complete destruction of the city by fire, and at least two of these streets were retained when the process of rebuilding began. One of these was the *Via Decumena* which ran from Cornhill, across the Walbrook, to Ludgate Hill. The road leading from this thoroughfare to the bridge across the Thames leading to Southwark was also preserved in the new street plan. Since this new venture was a joint one between the government and private finance, one might have expected the buildings which were erected after the fire to be a good deal grander and more substantial than those destroyed by Boudica. One would be right. With government money flowing into the area, the new London was very different from the city that it replaced. This was reflected not just in the size and type of the buildings but in the very materials used in their construction.

To protect the new city, a fortified military camp was established on the north bank of the Thames. This was surrounded with a deep ditch and pro-tected by timber and turf walls, making use of charred beams salvaged from the ruins of Londinium. Pieces of leather tents have been found, as well as the remains of a granary and cookhouse. This military camp lasted for something like 25 years; until, in fact, it was quite sure that there would be no further assault on the city such as that made by Boudica. Engineers were drafted into London after the Boudican revolt and a massive new quay built. So well made is this that it is very unlikely that it was a product of private initiative. Having decided to turn London into the capital, the powers that be were prepared to commit their own money and manpower to ensure the success of the rebuilding. It was a matter of Roman prestige that the city rose again, bigger and better than before from the ashes of its destruction.

The new city was to be Roman in every respect. If both the governor and procurator would be living here, they could hardly live in wattle-and-daub shacks with earthen floors and no furniture! Not only would such august personages require properly built houses, they and the other officials would need all the comforts and diversions of any other Roman city: bath-houses, amphitheatre and so on. Now it might be possible to put together an amphitheatre from timber and earth. In fact, that is exactly what the first amphitheatre was made of when it was constructed in about AD 70. Common sense, though, tells us that a bathhouse with a furnace and hypoc-aust will not last long if it is built of wood. Clearly, stone will be needed for such a place. Other important sites would also need stone: the governor's palace, the forum, temples, fort and monuments.

There has always been a problem for Londoners wishing to build in stone. There are chalk ridges south of the Thames, the nearest being the hills over-looking the river at Greenwich. Chalk has been used for building; the walls of the crypt of London's oldest church, All Hallows by the Tower, are made of chalk blocks. Chalk is fine for small-scale work, but it is too soft for larger structures. It can be scratched by fingernails and wears away very quickly. We need to travel a little further afield if we want to find hard stone suitable for cutting into blocks and using for walls. Stone is heavy and transporting it by road is an arduous and time-consuming task. The Romans were fairly familiar with Kent by this time and had found outcrops of a limy sandstone known as Kentish ragstone there. One ragstone quarry in particular was ideally situated for exploitation by London builders. It was near the town of Maidstone, next to the River Medway. What this meant in practical terms was that stone could be cut, loaded on to ships moored in the Medway and then taken up past Rochester and Chatham to the Thames. From there, it was literally plain sailing to London itself.

Most of the important buildings of Roman London were made of Kentish ragstone. The wall round the city that went up at the end of the second century was of the same material. We know quite a bit about the way in which stone was brought from Kent to London. On 6 September 1962, a Roman shipwreck was found at Blackfriars in central London. A bronze coin fixed beneath the mast when the boat was built enables us to date it to the second century. It was loaded with 26 tons of Kentish ragstone and had evidently sunk after a collision with another ship. I said that this was a Roman ship, but that is a debateable point. The construction of the ship seemed to have more in common with traditional Celtic techniques, rather than what we know of Roman shipbuilding. It suggests that the trafficking of stone from the quarries of Maidstone to the building sites in London may have been carried out by British workers hiring themselves out to the occupiers.

The use of stone for civic buildings in the capital did not mean that everybody else stopped using wattle-and-daub or wooden planks for their homes. Even at its height, Roman London was a city of wood rather than stone. Thatched roofs would always be cheaper than terracotta tiles. There were subtle differences though in the new city as opposed to that which first grew here in the immediate aftermath of the invasion. This was essentially a planned city. It might have been the case that any itinerant carpenter could have fetched up on Cornhill in AD 50, knocked up a roundhouse and opened for business. This was most decidedly not how things were now that the governor was based here. There was town planning and what the Americans call 'zoning', with some districts being designated commercial or industrial, while others were purely residential. After all, the governor would not want some shanty town to spring up next to his palace or for access to the bathhouse to be obstructed by squatters.

Central to the city was what archaeologists call the 'proto-forum'. This was a complex of stone buildings surrounding a central courtyard. It occupied the top of Cornhill in roughly the same place where the original army camp would have been, north of Fenchurch Street and Lombard Street. This public square and the offices around it was built in AD 70 and stood for perhaps 50 years. It measured about 300ft in length. It was ultimately replaced in the second century by a basilica and forum about four times as large. One of the things we notice about the city in the 30 or 40 years after its re-founding is that a number of the most prominent places such as the amphitheatre and forum were put up in a hurry and then later demolished to make way for a better or more permanent version.

Both the character of the new city and also the extent to which it would be a welcoming environment for the natives of the country was determined to a great extent by the personality of the governor who had his residence in the city. In the aftermath of the Boudican revolt, Suetonius Paulinus, the then governor, wreaked a ferocious vengeance upon the country. In the long run, this was likely to prove counter-productive and liable to stir up another rebellion. Suetonius rampaged around East Anglia, massacring those tribes who either supported Boudica's insurgency or had remained neutral. According to at least one contemporary historian, there were many Britons who were still prepared to resist and if Suetonius had been allowed to continue unchecked, another revolt could easily have erupted. That this did not in fact happen was largely due to one man; the new procurator.

Perhaps a few words about the post of procurator might be helpful at this point. Shifting 40,000 soldiers to Britain kept them and their commanders from intriguing in mainland Europe and plotting some sort of coup against the leadership in Rome. It created, though, a new problem, in that a man with 40,000 troops at his command, stationed on an island separate from Europe, might begin to get a little ambitious in other directions. He might, for instance, decide to declare himself independent form Rome. This actually happened in later centuries, as we shall see. A way round this was to split the power in provinces, by giving the military command to one man and financial control to another. The procurator of a province held the purse strings. Since the army's loyalty depended heavily upon being paid regularly, this gave the procurator a certain amount of influence in military affairs. Having two men, each jealous of the other's power, made it less likely that there would be a unified attempt to seize power in a province; it was classic divide and rule. When once this useful arrangement fell into abeyance, the trouble started in Britain.

It will be recalled that the man who was procurator at the time of Boudica's revolt fled to the continent by sea. He was replaced by a man called Julius Classicianus. The interesting thing to note about the new procurator is that he was himself of Celtic stock and therefore likely to have more sympathy with the harried tribes of Essex and Norfolk than would a pure Roman. The situation for those living in the south-east of Britain was grim enough, even without the revenge being taken by the Roman army. As they expected to be able to take over the army's granaries if their uprising was successful, the Iceni and other tribes who fought in AD 60 had not planted their crops that year. They faced therefore the spectre of starvation. Classicianus sent messages to Rome, complaining of Suetonius' brutal treatment of those living to the north and east of London. An official inquiry was held and the result was that a new governor was appointed to Britain.

As far as Classicianus and the new governor were concerned, the aim now was to be reconciliation, with Romans and Britons living side by side in the new capital and the culture of Rome providing an unifying glue which held their society together. If the Britons chose to live in the new city, learn Latin and adopt the toga, then they would be treated as fully the equal of the native-born Roman. This policy was continued and indeed made even more explicit under Agricola, who became governor of Britain in AD 77.

As we approach the year AD 100, Roman London is starting to look more like most people's idea of a Roman city. Although the great majority of buildings are still of wattle-and-daub or wood, they are often painted white. The civic buildings and some others have roofs made of red tiles. This is no shanty town which has grown organically on the fringe of a temporary army camp, but a properly planned and well-run city in the Roman style.

The first settlement on the twin hills of Cornhill and Ludgate sprang up almost by accident. A motley crew of Britons, Gaulish traders, adventurers and shady characters flocked to the port to see what profit there was to be made from the new province. This would have given the first incarnation of London a very cosmopolitan air, with various nationalities rubbing shoulders, united only in the desire to make a quick buck. The new London which rose from the ashes of the old was a different affair entirely. This was always going to be a purely Roman city. That is not to say that there were no other nationalities living and working here, but if they stayed for long, then they would generally be expected to conform to the mores of civilised, that is to say Roman, society.

4

Londinium at its Peak

Between AD 122, when the emperor Hadrian visited Britain, and the Antonine Plague which decimated the Roman Empire from AD 165 onwards, Roman London attained its greatest geographical extent. It may theoretically have been wealthier in later centuries, but London certainly was at its physical peak in the middle of the second century AD.

Second-century London had all the trappings and much of the external appearance of a typical Roman city: the baths, the amphitheatre, a basilica, forum and grand government offices. Although the great majority of the buildings were still of wood, they mostly had a coat of whitewash on the outside. This made the place look brighter and cleaner. Some roofs were thatched, but many were now tiled. The roof tiles and bricks used by the Romans were nothing more than clay, shaped and fired in a kiln. London is built upon clay and if you want a limitless supply, it is only necessary to dig down a dozen feet or so.

Regular supplies of stone were also entering the city by boat from Kent. This meant that important buildings such as the basilica, amphitheatre and bathhouses could be stone built. This too gave London a more solid and civilised look. In the early days of the city, before it had been destroyed by Boudica, there had been quite a few traditional Celtic roundhouses, especially on the outskirts of the town. These had gone. Anybody wishing to live and work in London during the second century was expected to conform in every respect to Roman ideas of what was appropriate for a city.

Perhaps the most noticeable building in the whole city was the basilica. This was enormous; perhaps the largest building outside Italy itself. In the last chapter we saw that the first forum had been built at the crest of

Cornhill, in the highest part of the city. In AD 90, work began on a new basilica and forum, which would eventually replace the old one. The first one remained open during this work. It was a massive undertaking and the building work took over 30 years to complete. There is reason to suppose that when Hadrian visited London in AD 122 he made some observations of the new basilica's design and suggested ways that it could be improved. There is at any rate clear evidence that a change of plan was adopted half-way through its construction; a time which would fit neatly in with the emperor's visit.

The new forum was about four times as large as the old one. Indeed, so great was it that it proved possible to build the new complex around the old one. As the new forum went up, the old one was left standing in what would eventually become the central courtyard. Once the new basilica and surrounding offices and shops were finished, all that was then needed was to knock down the old one, smooth over the ground and then put the finishing touches to the new forum with an archway and fourth row of buildings to finish off and enclose the forum on all sides.

The forum which emerged from all this work was over 300ft long. Its size reflected London's own increased population and importance as the provincial capital. The basilica which stood on the north side of the forum served as combined law courts and town hall. The town council met here and legal matters were also dealt with in the same place. It was a three-storey building and would have been visible from almost any part of the city. Some of the foundations of this enormous building may still be seen. The walls were built of stone brought into London from the quarries in Maidstone. The basilica formed one side of a large open square, in which a market was held. Shops and offices lined the square and these were protected by a col-onnaded veranda. This was the Roman equivalent of a shopping mall. It was a place to hang out and meet one's friends; perhaps catch up with the gossip.

Quite a few houses had to be demolished to make room in the city centre for the new forum. As we saw, its construction took place over a period of perhaps 30 years. Despite the extensive planning which apparently went into the building of this complex, it was beset with problems throughout its existence. Almost as soon as it was finished, cracks appeared due to subsid-ence and over the next century and a half various repairs and modifications were made. Following the decline in population in London which took place as the second century drew on, the office space around the forum proved surplus to requirements and some of it was unused for many years.

There were other civic buildings in London. Beneath Cannon Street railway station lie the remains of a large public building. This may have been the official residence of the governor of Britain or it might equally well just be a civil service office block. There is no way of telling at this late date. This, like the basilica, was built on a grand scale. For some years, it was assumed that this enormous building, which covered 3.5 acres, could only have been the official residence of the governor of Britain. More recent investigations have raised the suspicion that it was not one huge palace at all, but rather a linked series of offices. It consisted in part of an 80ft-long hall, with accommodation probably provided for guests in wings on either side. An enormous ornamental pond lay in front of the hall, over a hundred feet long. Even this pond was constructed on a monumental scale, lying upon a raft of concrete 6ft thick. Whatever its purpose, this building was certainly meant to impress with its opulence.

The complex beneath Cannon Street station faces a similar building on the other side of the Thames at Southwark. The remains of this building were found near the site of the medieval Winchester Palace and they too could possibly be the residence of somebody important. On the other hand, they might also be no more than administrative headquarters, perhaps with a military connection. We shall look more closely at this structure in the chapter on Southwark.

What changes would the ordinary Londoner have seen, comparing the first pre-Boudican city and the one which Hadrian visited in AD 122? The most important change is that London was now, in the early second century, a Roman city. What do we mean when we describe something as being 'Roman'? Are we talking about a nationality? A geographical origin? A style? In fact being 'Roman', whether this adjective is applied to a man or city, was more a frame of mind than anything else. We talk freely of 'Roman' governors, 'Roman' soldiers and 'Roman' cities; it is time to consider carefully what we mean by the adjective 'Roman' in this context.

In the last chapter we met Julius Alpinus Classicianus, the Roman procurator who was appointed to London in the aftermath of the Boudican revolt. Here was an important 'Roman' official whose complaints about the governor, Suetonius Paulinus, led to his being withdrawn from the province entirely. In what sense was Julius Classicianus a 'Roman'? He was a Celt by birth who had been born in what is now France. As far as we know, he had never even been to Rome. And yet to the Roman administration, his word was as good as any native-born Roman's and he had been able to rise to the highest office in the province of Britain.

Julius Classicianus was by no means unusual in being able to rise high in the Roman system while not having been born in Rome or even Italy itself. The army and civil service across the empire were full of such men. During the second century, the 'Roman' governors of Britain who had their headquarters in London actually came from places as varied as Africa, Turkey, Yugoslavia and Spain. In the army stationed in this country, a legionary commander called Claudius Charax was a Greek-speaking man from modern-day Turkey, while officers under his command were drawn from France, Germany and Egypt. There was no suggestion at all that being 'Roman' meant having to come from Rome.

This concept applied equally to the British. Tacitus tells that his father-in-law Agricola, who was the governor of Britain in the late first century, encouraged the Britons to adopt Roman habits such as the wearing of the toga and speaking Latin. By doing so, they effectively became as Roman as anybody else. In short, attempting to draw a distinction between the men from Rome living in London and Britons who were wearing togas and speaking in Latin is quite meaningless: they were all Romans.

It is interesting, apropos of the idea of 'Roman-ness', to look at the graffiti found in both London and the rest of the province during the later years of the occupation. One might reasonably assume that monumental inscriptions would be in Latin or dedications in temples. What is revealing is that even the graffiti of working men, brief comments scratched on a tile or unglazed clay jar, are also in Latin. No graffiti has been found in Celtic, suggesting strongly that ordinary people in the cities used Latin for their day-to-day language. One would have heard Latin spoken in the streets of first-century London, but this would not indicate in the least where a man had actually been born and brought up. Those living in London wished to be civilised, to be Roman, and that meant using Latin not only in day-to-day conversation, but also even if they wished to scratch a funny remark about a workmate on the wall of his shop.

Thus, anybody walking around early second-century London, about the time of Hadrian's visit, would be sure to see more togas in the streets and hear far more Latin being spoken that would have been the case had he visited London before the Boudican destruction. Apart from that, what other changes would one have noticed? The buildings would have been a bit brighter, with more of them whitewashed. Wooden walkways would have lined the streets, so that shoppers would not need to walk through the mud. The variety of goods on sale would be far greater. As they became 'Roman', the citizens of London would have naturally begun to eat a more Mediterranean diet than before. Beer would be out and wine in. Olive oil would be used in cooking in preference to sheep fat. Olives would be imported from Europe along with many other unfamiliar foods. One shipwreck in this country contained an amphora with 6000 olive stones inside. Clearly, olives were a big hit here at that time.

The city would have been every bit as noisy as it was in the first years. Rome was, as we have seen, a very noisy place and London would have been even worse. There might now be bathhouses and the taking of regular baths was de rigueur for those who wished to be civilised, but even that would have a downside, especially for those living nearby. The bathhouses were very noisy places and living near one would have been as undesirable for the Roman Londoner as living next door to a pub or nightclub would be for us today. Seneca, the philosopher, tells us what it was like to live near such a place in Rome. He said that 'the sound of voices is enough to make one sick'. He goes on to provide a vivid and detailed description of the racket that came from such places: the sound of men exercising with weights, the noise of brawls, men calling the score in ball games, splashing, shouting, the cries of the sausage sellers. It is unlikely that living near the fort or amphitheatre would have been any quieter or even just near a row of shops. Roman London was small, but it was noisy.

Suppose we went into a typical home at this time. What improvements might we have seen in the domestic lifestyle? Fewer floors made simply of pounded earth or puddled clay would be one thing that we would spot at once. That is not to say that every house one entered would have glorious, polychrome mosaics showing Orpheus and Eurydice or the rape of the Sabine women! More common would be plain red tesserae floors. These are made up of little cubes of stone set in cement. Colour Plate 9 shows such a floor. It is not a brilliant piece of craftsmanship; the cubes are placed in crooked lines and it is not particularly pleasing from an aesthetic point of view. It is, however, vastly preferable to bare earth. An even more popular type of flooring was *opus signum*. This consisted of small bits of broken pottery and fragments of old tiles set in mortar and pounded flat. It was extremely cheap to produce, which was part of its attraction. In his *Natural History*, Pliny mentions *opus signum* as being very popular for floors; he says: 'Even broken pottery has been utilized; it being found that, beaten to powder, and tempered with lime, it becomes more solid and durable than other substances of a similar nature; forming the cement known as the "*Signine*" composition, so extensively employed for even making the pavements of houses.'

Colour Plate 10 shows a piece of such flooring from a London house. The internal walls of the home would probably be painted, although plain whitewash would be far more likely than an elaborate fresco of the sort we see in the houses at Pompeii.

During the pre-Boudican phase of the city, cooking was often carried out on fires built in the middle of the floor. Now, we are more likely to find a custom-built stove or oven. Some of the larger houses might have had hypocausts – clay pipes which conducted the heat of a furnace into the floors and walls. This would be very rare, though, in a private home. More common would be a portable charcoal brazier. This could be moved around the home, depending upon where the heat was most needed. There were hazards, however, in this sort of heating. Windows were now more likely to be fitted with glass. It might have been rough, translucent glass, as opposed to modern, clear, float glass, but it would still keep out drafts and let in the light. The problem was that burning charcoal produces carbon monoxide and that, in an enclosed and unventilated space, is lethal. At least two Roman emperors are known to have died from this cause.

Lighting would have been provided more by lamps fuelled with olive oil than was the case a few decades earlier. Olive oil had changed from being an exotic luxury to an essential household commodity, used for both cooking and lighting. Colour Plate 11 shows the kind of oil lamp which was becoming very popular at this time.

We have seen that London in the first century had many of the amenities which Romans regarded as being essential basics: the amphitheatre, the baths and so on. One feature was conspicuously lacking and this is surprising in view of the city's recent history. There were no walls. One might have thought that after Boudica swept into the unprotected city in AD 60 and razed it to the ground, some thought might have been given to defence. True, a fort had been built which might perhaps have housed a thousand soldiers, but the city itself was as wide open in the second century as it had been in the first.

As we saw, for the first 25 years after the attack by Boudica, a fortified military camp was operating on the north bank of the Thames and the plan may well have been that in the event of another revolt, the citizens of London would come into the camp for protection. After 20 years or so, it would be fairly obvious that any future disturbances were likely to be in the north of the country rather than near London. One form of defence was constructed around the city, but it was exceedingly limited. An earth bank with a ditch at the front marked the city limits. This was very similar to the arrangements around the British *oppida* when the Romans first landed. In this country, chariots continued to be used in warfare long after they had been abandoned in mainland Europe. Boudica's forces contained many chariots; it is how we remember her best, from the statue in Westminster. A bank and ditch surrounding a settlement would prevent the chariots from getting too close. Of course, it would provide no protection against determined men scrambling across, but at least horses and chariots could be left out of the equation.

Almost all reconstructions of Roman London, whether they are artists' impressions in children's history books or models in museums, show Roman London on the north bank of the Thames. Anything south of the river is sketchily indicated as a small cluster of houses. In recent years, evidence has been emerging that the part of Roman London which lay on the other side of the River Thames might have been more important than has generally been thought. It is time now to look in detail at Roman Southwark and the role it played in the development of the city.

5

Southwark

There is among those who live in what one might term 'London proper' (which is to say the City of London, Westminster and the suburbs north, west and east of these districts) a certain amount of snobbishness about that half of London which lies on the other side of the River Thames. The river forms a powerful psychological barrier and an eastender will refer to Southwark or Bermondsey as 'south of the river' or even 'across the water'. With a dozen bridges crossing the Thames in central London and five different underground lines running beneath it, there is no rational justification for regarding the river flowing through London as anything other than an imaginary line somewhat like the equator. Still, there it is. Those in north London do rather regard south London as being a barbarous wilderness. It is amusing to speculate as to whether this is a leftover cultural relic, an exceedingly ancient folk memory perhaps, of the time before the Roman invasion when the Thames was a national border between the tribes of the Cantiaci in the south and Catuvellauni across the river in the north.

It is not impossible that this north London chauvinism has been partly responsible for the lack of interest shown in Roman Southwark until fairly recently. It has in the past been suggested that the development of this part of London occurred at a later stage than that on Cornhill and Ludgate Hill. We now know that this is quite untrue and that the settlements on both sides of the Thames were founded at the same time and began to grow together as soon as Claudius' soldiers arrived in the area.

It might help if we were to think for a moment about the nature of Southwark at the time of the Roman invasion. As with the rest of London, we are used to dry streets and our experience of the river is often limited to an occasional glimpse from the top deck of a bus; we tend to forget that London was historically a city of rivers. Most Londoners have heard vaguely of the Fleet and Walbrook, but not many know of the ancient rivers which once flowed through south London: the Neckinger, Peck, Effra and Quaggy River. Today, these rivers are known only by the districts and streets to which they have bequeathed their names, such as Peckham and Effra Road in Brixton. Their influence on the early settlers of London was, however, profound.

The Effra, its name meaning 'torrent' in Celtic, entered the Thames near Westminster. The Quaggy River meandered through Greenwich. To understand Roman Southwark, it is the Neckinger at which we must look. When rivers enter the sea or flow into a larger river, they do so in one of two ways. Either they widen slightly and form an estuary or they break into a number of little streams and form a delta. The River Fleet widened to an estuary 600ft long when it entered the Thames at Blackfriars. The Tyburn, on the other hand, formed a delta which divided the land around Westminster into two or three islands surrounded by marshland. South of the Thames, the Neckinger also formed a delta.

The Thames was far wider than it is today, and at high tide there was nothing at all to stop it flowing freely into a series of creeks, inlets and streams. The whole of Southwark was inundated, with the exception of two or three gravel islands roughly where London Bridge railway station is now. At high tide, Southwark became an archipelago; at low tide it was a network of swamps and fenland. Southwark was of strategic importance in the years following the invasion of Claudius, as the place where the road from Kent reached the lowest crossing point of the Thames. We shall look later in this chapter at the bridge which was built across the Thames, but the Roman army's first exercise in bridge building in this new province would probably have been not the Thames but the Neckinger.

It would be impractical to march troops across rivers and through swamps on a regular basis and so even to reach the south bank of the Thames would have needed some kind of bridge. If nothing else, we know that Claudius brought elephants with him for a grand entry into Colchester. If they landed in Kent, then these creatures would need to have been brought through Southwark at some point. The idea of these great animals being led through mudflats and marshes is frankly absurd. Some sort of arrangement must have been made to get them through Southwark.

All this argues for early activity by Roman engineers in this part of London. The dry ground nearest to the Thames at this point is Duke Street

Hill and it is a reasonable guess that the army must have set up a marching camp here to supervise and facilitate the crossing of the Thames by other troops. According to Roman historians, the army which entered the area in AD 43 was unable to find the ford that Caesar's forces used in 54 BC and used instead a bridge. We do not know whether or not this was a pre-existing bridge built by the Celts; it is more likely to have been a wooden pontoon erected quickly by engineers. We know from their campaigns in Europe that this would not have been a very tricky problem for the Roman army. There are records of a number of occasions when they did precisely this in Gaul.

Whether it has been caused by the same kind of rivalry between north and south London which I mentioned above, or whether it is simply that there are more archaeologists working north of the Thames than there are in south London, the fact is that the Roman history of Southwark has been neglected over the years. Until fairly recently, any reconstruction of Roman London would show only the area north of the Thames. This was, after all, the walled city, containing all the forum, fort, basilica, amphitheatre, governor's palace and so on. What on earth could there have been worth looking at across the river? In fact, recent work has revealed quite a few things worth examining in Roman Southwark and the more that this area is excavated, the important it becomes in understanding Roman London in general.

Pre-Roman tracks, which would later be developed by the Romans into metalled roads and become famous as Watling Street, led from Kent to London and then north into the Midlands. The original track certainly crossed the Thames at Westminster, where there was a ford and during the Bronze Age a bridge. It is likely that this ford remained in use during the early years of the Roman occupation, but a crossing a little closer to the main part of the new settlement of Londinium would soon have been needed. This means that Watling Street soon crossed the Thames not at Westminster but a few yards to the east of London Bridge, connecting Southwark to the main area of London on Cornhill. The first permanent bridge was built here within a decade of the invasion. This in itself would be enough to ensure the importance of Southwark – that it was the first part of London that travellers landing in Kent would encounter. It would also give Southwark a strategic importance in a purely military sense – that of the need to guard and protect one end of the bridge.

During the 1990s, the Jubilee underground line was extended through Southwark. This gave archaeologists the chance to investigate in greater detail than had been possible in the past precisely what lay under Southwark. Something which became immediately apparent was that Southwark too had been razed during the Boudican revolt. The same 'red layer' or Boudican Destruction Horizon was evident here as in the City of London proper. This was intriguing.

First, the 'red layer' showed that Southwark must have been large enough in AD 60 to provoke the rebels into crossing the bridge to torch it. In fact, the 'red layer' covered a considerable area, a far greater area than had previously been thought must have been built up here in the first century. Secondly, the warriors following Boudica must have planned the destruction of London in a methodical fashion. If they had simply arrived and set fire to everything, then they might not later have been able to get to Southwark to burn it. Clearly, they must have started setting fire to Southwark and only then begun burning the city on the north bank of Thames.

The more that Roman Southwark is investigated in this way, the more its importance emerges. Two examples will illustrate this.

The medieval bishops of Winchester had a palace in Southwark. It became obscured by warehouses and other buildings, but the great hall can now be seen again, including a rose window; minus, of course, its glass. Archaeological excavations beneath here in 1983, brought to light a Roman building. This was no ordinary building, but a very large and prestigious one with an under-floor heating system and perhaps a bathhouse. This was not a private house; it was far too grand for that. The best guess was that it was the administrative centre for some organisation. It was unlikely to have been connected with the running of the city, because we know that the basilica and possibly governor's palace were to be found across the river in the City of London.

There were clues to this important buildings function and history. A marble tablet was unearthed which listed various military units. This led some to speculate that the military headquarters for London was based here, rather than across the Thames. A more radical idea was that this was in fact the command base for the navy, the Roman equivalent of the Admiralty. It has even been suggested that this building might have been the headquarters of the procurator. Some very fine wall paintings were also recovered, unique in London. All that we can say with confidence is that this was an important public building which indicates that Roman Southwark was not a backwater of the main settlement of London, but important in its own right.

The above idea of the importance of Southwark was reinforced during the digging of the foundations for an office block near Borough High

Street. This led in 2002 to the discovery of the largest temple complex found in the London area. Some time in the second century, an area of Roman Southwark was cleared of houses, levelled and used as the site of two temples and other associated buildings. This complex was surrounded by a wall to make a sacred enclosure or *temenos*. Apart from the temples, there was also another building which has tentatively been identified as a guesthouse or inn, where travellers or worshippers could stay for the night. In the area of the *temenos* were three plinths which once supported either altars or cult statues.

The presence of such a complex as this on the other side of the river from the main city gives us an idea of the importance of this district. Even more galling for snobbish Londoners on the other side of the Thames, this site also yielded the earliest written mention of Londoners ever to be found. A marble plaque is addressed to 'the people of London' and dedicated the temples to Mars-Camulos.

One final indicator which might suggest that Southwark was a substantial district and important in its own right is that it had its own cemetery. This was excavated in 1996.

Southwark would from the very first days of the Claudian invasion have been a place of strategic importance. The road from Kent arrived at this point on the Thames and both banks of the crossing would have needed to be secured and guarded by troops. It has been strongly suspected since the early nineteenth century that the first bridge over the Thames built by the Romans would have been roughly where London Bridge stands. When work began on building the new London Bridge in 1824, the riverbed was dredged and many Roman remains were found. It seemed clear that this was where the Roman bridge had been. The question which nobody could answer was when it had been built. In 1981, the remains of a pier base for the Roman bridge was found. This was dated by dendrochronology to no earlier than AD 85.

It is fairly obvious that some sort of crossing was established at Southwark a lot earlier than 40 years after the invasion of AD 43. It has been suggested that at first a ferry operated here, but that is unlikely. By AD 45, the roads to London from the south of Britain converged at that part of Southwark which roughly corresponds to Duke Street Hill and it is plain that many people were entering the main settlement of London here. We also have contemporary accounts of some sort of bridge being in use near here during the invasion itself. It has been hypothesised that this may have been a military pontoon bridge; a floating wooden arrangement of a sort used in other places by the Roman army. As far as the theory of a ferry goes, this is not really tenable. When Boudica and her people attacked London and burned it to the ground, are we really supposed to believe that in order to loot and destroy Southwark, they rowed backwards and forwards across the river in small groups?

All other considerations aside, we know that docks were built at Southwark and that it was a busy part of the port of London. The same process was taking place here as one the other side of the river; that of slowly containing the Thames within more clearly defined boundaries and thus making the banks less marshy. Over the centuries, quays and jetties were constructed on the opposite sides of the Thames at London. When new quays were made, this was done by moving forward for a distance and advancing the river bank, so reclaiming more land. The more that this was done, the less soggy the built-up parts of Roman London became. Some of London, the area along the Walbrook valley for example, was notoriously marshy and the buildings there prone to damp and subsidence. Gradually, as the River Thames was squeezed more and more and moved further from the city itself, the situation improved. In Colour Plate 12 we can see what the bridge and docks might have looked at this time, when London's maritime trade was at its height.

Something very noticeable about the successive dockland areas which were constructed on reclaimed land is that each is a little lower than the one before. There is a reason for this. The level of the Thames itself was dropping and so each new jetty had to be built a little lower than the ones constructed a few years earlier. This had profound, one might almost say catastrophic, effects upon London's commercial vitality by the middle of the fourth century. We shall examine this idea later on.

We have looked at the physical nature of Roman London and seen how it changed in the course of a century or so. We have also seen what the home life of Londoners might have been like over the course of this period. It is time now to consider what people were actually doing in the city. Where did they work; what did they do with their spare time? In the next chapter we shall try to get as feel for the lives of those living in the city which we have been describing.

6

Recreation and Work

Some places are famous for what is found there and others are renowned for what they produce. South Africa, for example, has many diamonds which are waiting to be dug from the earth. Switzerland, on the other hand, is well known for the clocks and watches which are manufactured there using metal mined elsewhere in the world. London has few natural resources other than water and mud. Unfortunately, the demand for these two commodities has never been sufficiently great in other parts of the world to make their export a commercially viable undertaking. The genius of London has accordingly always been for financial dealing and trading in raw materials and manufactured goods produced elsewhere. In this country 'the City' is synonymous with business dealings.

That this was so even in the earliest years of London's existence is indicated by a passage in Tacitus' biography of his father-in-law, the statesman Agricola. He writes that London was 'full of merchants and a famous centre for commerce'. The precise words which he chooses are significant. He says: '*copia negotiatorum et commeatuum maxime celebre.*' The word he uses for merchants, *negotiatores*, is invariably applied to those dealing in financial speculations such as money lending, rather than simple trade or the buying and selling of commodities. Had this been what he wished to imply, he would undoubtedly have used the expression '*mercatores*', meaning tradesmen. It is safe to assume that within 20 or 30 years of its founding, London was well known for being at the centre of the money markets.

We shall return to this subject in a little while, but before we do so, perhaps we should look in general at the economic structure of Roman London. At its height, the city had many thousand inhabitants. They could not all have made a living from lending money to each other!

A lot of the study of history involves political theory, accounts of military campaigns and the domestic life of the wealthy and famous. Before history of this sort can even begin though, people need to have somewhere to live and food to eat. The small section of the Thames valley which later became the city of London was more or less a blank canvas for the invading Romans. Before any sort of 'history' could take place or anybody could even think about lending money to anybody else or selling them anything, it would first be necessary to have somewhere to live. This at once gives us a surprising insight into the type of work which would inevitably have dominated the first years of London's existence. This is a type of enterprise with which one does not immediately associate city life, namely logging.

In Chapter 2, we looked at the sort of homes that the early Londoners lived in. They were made of wood, coated with mud or clay and with roofs of dried grass or reeds. The sheer quantity of wood that Roman London required throughout the 400 years or so of its existence is staggering. Even when the city had been built, mainly of wood but partly of stone, a vast amount of wood was still needed for the day-to-day running of the place. There were two main communal bathhouses, one in Cheapside and one near the Thames on Huggin Hill. The furnaces in these establishments were kept burning 24 hours a day. This was more economical than letting the fires die down at night and restarting them early the next morning. Each of these baths would have used annually about 50 or 60 acres of woodland. This would mean that those two bathhouses alone would be responsible for the deforestation of an area of land every three years roughly the size of London's Hyde Park. From early autumn to late spring, every single resident of the city would also rely upon the burning of wood to warm their homes and cook their food. The cooking fires would be maintained throughout the summer as well. Enormous quantities of timber were also needed for building the docks, the wooden walkways in the streets and for the scaffolding needed to erect stone buildings. More would be needed to fuel the kilns which produced bricks and roof tiles for the city. The logging operations needed to supply this demand were enormous.

We are, however, running ahead of ourselves a little. In London's first years, the little settlement which began to grow up around the marching camp on Cornhill would need to build homes for themselves. These typically combined both business premises and residential accommodation. The first step would be to chop down trees and prepare the trunks into planks and posts. This meant that there was a great demand for unskilled labourers in the early years: men to dig and haul; to wield axes and saws; to dig ditches and lay tracks through the forests. These same manual labourers would be employed in erecting posts, mixing mud and clay, clearing the sites for new buildings – all the rough work that is today still undertaken by brawny young men on building sites and in logging camps. It is a fair guess that most of this work would be undertaken by Britons who would perhaps hire themselves out. Certainly some of the Romans who were around at this time would have had slaves with them, but nowhere near enough to provide the manpower needed to build a city. Besides, this was dangerous work. If one owned a valuable slave, one would not simply allow him to be used as general labourer in a logging camp. The situation would be far more like that which arises when a building project is carried out by the Americans or British today in a less economically developed nation. The planning, which is specialised work, is undertaken by experts and the donkey work is done by cheap labour from the surrounding area.

This building boom would have gone on for years. By AD 60, London may have had as many as 10,000, perhaps even 20,000, inhabitants; all living and working in wooden buildings erected since AD 43. There would also have been a need for iron nails, saws, axes and other tools. Some of these would have been imported from continental Europe, but of course the British also made their own tools. There must have been forges operating as soon as the building work began to make and repair tools. A skilled British blacksmith might well move to the area with his family to take advantage of the constant stream of work available. As the community grew, they would need food and this would be brought in from the surrounding countryside. While all the building work for accommodation was taking place, docks would also be going up. Ships would soon be arriving with cargoes of Roman food and drink; wine, olives and *liquamen*, the fish sauce which was their equivalent of tomato sauce, to be spread liberally on practically anything they ate.

The economic exploitation of the new province began almost as soon as the Romans had pacified a district. Lead was being mined and cast into ingots for export. This would need decent roads to bring it by cart from the mines and load it into ships. Warehouses would be needed to keep goods safe from pilfering. We know that the mining of lead and its export to Europe began very soon after the conquest of Britain; certainly at least 10 years before the Boudican revolt. We know this because lead bars have been found with the following inscription: TI•CLAVD•CAESAR•AVG•P•M•TR•P•VIIII •IMP•XVI•DE•BRITAN. Roughly translated, this means: 'For Tiberius Claudius

Caesar Augustus; High Priest, holding Tribune's powers for the ninth time, hailed Imperator in the field sixteen times; from Britain.' All of which means that this particular ingot of lead must have been cast in either AD 48 or 49. Consignments of this metal, as well as the silver which was extracted at the same time, must have been passing through London from the very earliest years of the occupation.

The opportunities for work in London, even for an uneducated and illiterate Briton, would have been limitless. For many young people, men and women, this new city would have been a lot more exciting than the quiet villages in which they had grown up. This was where it was happening; this was the place to be. We know that at least one street of shops was operating in London within a short time of the founding of the city. This street ran east to west, parallel with modern-day Lombard Street and Cheapside. By AD 47, a drain had been installed along the middle of this street, channelling a small tributary of the Walbrook. It was made of wood and could not have been laid later than AD 48, only five years after Claudius' forces first landed.

Once the basic framework of the city had been put into place – the houses and shops, drinking places and brothels, warehouses, docks, roads, workshops and stables – then the serious speculators would move in. These would be people with money to invest in prospecting and mining, money lending and other financial schemes. There were fortunes to be made in the new province and London was the place to make them. The Thames was directly opposite the mouth of the Rhine and ships were constantly skimming backwards and forwards across the North Sea. Another glance at the map in Colour Plate 8 will soon show why the businessmen who were intent on exploiting Britain chose London as their headquarters, rather than Colchester which was the nominal capital of the province. The network of roads which was beginning to spread across the country like a spider's web all centred upon London. If one wished to transport ingots of lead from Britain to Gaul, then the sooner one got them on board the ship, the better. The road from the lead mines of the Mendips heads straight to London. Why, after having transported your load overland that far, would you then choose to take it another 50 miles to Colchester in order to get it onto a ship? Why not just send it from London? The logic is inescapable and was fixed when Caesar and Claudius chose to land in Kent and work their way north-west, crossing the Thames at the ford near Westminster. It was this which decided the routes of the major roads which were subsequently built and this in turn made London more and more the logical choice for a port and trading centre.

There was one more thing which made London the perfect place for all the businessmen and financiers who came to Britain in the first years of the occupation. It has always been slightly puzzling that, with all the geographical advantages which the Roman port and city enjoyed, it had never occurred to the Celts to start some settlement here. After all, they were proficient seamen who quite happily popped two and fro across the Channel to visit their relatives. Why had no *oppidum* like that at Colchester grown up by the ford at Westminster? The Thames was not only a natural political or tribal border, it also had a deep religious significance; it was in effect a holy river like the Ganges or Jordan. People made votive offerings to the spirits or ancestors of the dead here. Places of that kind were often neutral areas for the prehistoric Britons; demilitarised zones, if you like. They did not belong to one tribe or another, but all were free to come and worship or sacrifice there. Here was a sacred zone which in any case lay between the territories of several tribes. Building a permanent settlement here would firstly have been a breach of the etiquette which was accepted for such places and would also have been viewed as an aggressive and expansionist action, liable to provoke war. One did not build one's towns right up against the border of another tribe, not unless one was looking for trouble.

All this meant that London was not really in any particular tribe's territory. It straddled the border. This was most definitely not the case with Colchester, which had been the de facto capital of the Trinovantes. Being based in London meant that one could just as easily trade with the natives of Kent as one could those of Hertfordshire or Essex. It was a central point both in a purely physical sense and also culturally. Plus, the building of it had not trodden on anybody's toes in the way that putting up a Roman temple in Colchester had done.

To whom did the money lenders based in London lend their money? Soldiers wanting a loan until payday would have been good 'bread and butter' business; particularly officers who had a lifestyle to maintain. No doubt many merchants and shopkeepers would also want to borrow money to buy new stock, tide them over until the next shipment arrived or because business was a little slack that month. There were other, bigger clients, though, and the lending of money to these bigger fish was to have catastrophic consequences which ultimately led to the ruin of the city. When I talk of ruin, I do not just mean financial ruin, but the physical liquidation of London and death of many of its inhabitants.

In Chapter 3, we saw the destruction of London by Boudica. She had gathered about her a force tens of thousands strong and destroyed utterly the cities of Colchester, London and St Albans; to say nothing of a number of smaller settlements such as Chelmsford. Boudica had, of course, powerful reasons for wishing to wreak death and destruction upon the Romans and all their works. There can be no doubt also that her humiliation at the hands of the occupiers provided the spark which set the south-east of the country ablaze and triggered an open call to arms. Nations and tribes seldom go to war purely and simply over one incident of this sort, no matter how disgusting. Those living in Essex and Norfolk already had grudges against the Romans. Their land had been seized and they had been evicted from their homes to make room for a lot of retired soldiers who behaved as though the native Britons were their slaves. There was also the fact that the military commander of the Roman army of occupation had gone to Wales so that he could invade and occupy the most sacred groves of the Druid priesthood on the Isle of Anglesey.

It is, of course, perfectly true that wars have in the past been fought solely over the question of religion, but these are rare. Far more common are conflicts which are precipitated because some nation or other feels itself to have been cheated or exploited. Most wars are fought not for noble and heroic reasons but over money. Machiavelli, that arch cynic, claimed that men will forgive and forget the death of their fathers before they do the loss of their inheritance. The leaders of the tribes in east Britain had good motives of their own for making common cause with Boudica and fighting to overthrow the Romans. It had nothing at all to do with either the violation of Boudica's daughters or the damage being done to the sacred groves of the Druids in far-off Wales. They stood to lose absolutely everything if the Roman occupation was not brought to an end.

As presented by the Romans in the immediate aftermath of the invasion, theirs was a mission of civilisation; they were bringing light into the darkness and were keen for the natives of Britain to join them on an equal footing in the new society which they were setting up. Of course, changing an entire way of life is not cheap and the acquisition of the trappings of civilisation would have to be paid for by those who wished to be raised up from their backwardness by the wise and enlightened men who had now assumed the running of their nation.

What sort of expenses are we talking about here? Building new towns in the Roman style, new villas for the chiefs, Roman food, educating themselves and their children in Latin, and the various arts and graces of civilisation; the list was a long one. Then there were the taxes, the new provincial council centred on Colchester – all this cost money. It cost so much money that the Celtic leaders really didn't know how they would be able to afford it. Which is, of course, where the Roman money lenders come into the picture.

Claudius had advanced large sums of money to tribes that had welcomed him rather than fighting. It had been assumed by those receiving this bounty that Claudius was their new friend and that he had arrived in Colchester with his war elephants for no other reason than to dish out money to them. This has seldom been the way of colonial occupiers! Roman money lenders, who had been some of the earliest businessmen to land in the new province after the invasion, had also lent very large amounts to the tribal leaders so that they could pay for Latin lessons, hire architects, buy wine and acquire all that they would need to become civilised in the Roman style.

In the months before the Boudican revolt broke out, the speculators in Rome and their agents in London, the money lenders themselves, began to put the bite on the Britons to repay all their loans at once. It must surely have been guessed that this would lead to ill feeling and perhaps provoke some chieftains to despair. There had already been one serious revolt in Gaul, caused by precisely the same thing. In AD 21 Florus and Sacrovir led their tribes against Rome. Their main complaint was the financial indebtedness which had been incurred by the borrowing of money from the Romans. The money lenders in London were often acting as middlemen on behalf of rich men in Rome. Seneca, Nero's old tutor, had a fortune invested in this way in Britain. It is possible that the Celts were not quite as savvy as the Romans on the implications of interest being charged on loans. They could not seem to understand how it was possible to borrow a large sum of money, pay back the full amount and yet still be in debt. In addition to the money which they had borrowed, they were now informed that the money which Claudius had dispensed so liberally when he arrived in Britain was not, as had been assumed, a free gift at all. This too would now have to be repaid.

The continuing military action in Britain must have made some of those in Rome uneasy about the fortunes that they had lent in this country. As so often happens in the world of finance, this uneasiness led to a panic which caused others to start calling in their loans too. The affair snowballed and resulted in the very thing of which everybody was afraid: defaulting on the loans. So much in the financial world depends in this way upon confidence and when a panic begins, it can be hard to halt. As the money lenders were pressing for full repayment of their loans, so the procurator was demanding that the money which Claudius had disbursed should now be returned to him. Faced with ruin and with creditors backed by the use of military force, it must have appeared to some of those tribal leaders that the answer to their difficulties might lie in renouncing the debts and killing those who were asking to be repaid.

A good case can be made for the money lenders operating in London during the first century AD having been responsible by their actions for the destruction of the city by Boudica. It is thought that when the city had been rebuilt, the money lending which subsequently took place was on a somewhat more modest scale. It would not be at all surprising if those with spare cash to invest abroad would think twice about becoming embroiled in another episode of this kind.

We have seen the kind of jobs which people had in Roman London. Even for a well-to-do shopkeeper, there would not be a great deal of spare time. For those who are working literally from dawn to dusk, and some-times longer, just to provide some sort of shelter and sufficient food to ward off starvation, the expression 'recreation' is probably not an appropriate one to describe the few hours when they are not actually working. Under such circumstances, a few hours' sleep and the freedom not to work are enough pleasure in themselves. It is likely that this was, by and large, the state of affairs in London before its destruction by Boudica in AD 60. Life was grim and few people had time for anything other than working, eating and sleep-ing. This changed, though, when the city was rebuilt and designated the capital of the province. A Roman city required Roman amusements and a way of life geared to something a little more satisfying than a mere struggle for survival in conditions roughly comparable to that of an undeveloped, third-world backwater.

Julius Agricola was appointed governor of Britain and arrived in the country in the summer of AD 77. It was the third time that he had been in Britain; he was almost certainly involved in suppressing Boudica's upris-ing 17 years earlier. Tacitus tells us of Agricola's campaign of what is best described as Romanisation. The natives of Britain should begin to enjoy the benefits of Roman civilisation and want more for themselves and their children than just grubbing out a miserable existence as subsistence farm-ers. The hope was to raise up the Britons to their own level and instil in them the love for those things which the Romans themselves held dear: art, literature, debate and the pleasures of civilised society in a city. These pleasures included both private amusements and communal activities. We shall look first at the diversions with which those living in London might have indulged themselves in their own homes.

Until a few decades ago, many people living in twentieth-century London would amuse themselves in the evenings by playing cards or competing with each other at a board game. Without television, internet, computer games or record players there was precious little else to do when sitting at home after work. Board games were a popular pastime too for those living in Roman London. Perhaps the most frequently played game was *Tabula*, which was a forerunner of backgammon. Roman dice and a shaker have been found in London, as well as bone gaming pieces. The object of *Tabula* was to move groups of counters around the board, making the moves in accordance with how three dice fell. This game seems to have aroused violent passions, possibly caused by the high stakes for which some people played. Just as with backgammon, *Tabula* could equally well be played for fun at home or in a tavern for ruinously high stakes. A wall painting in Pompeii shows in a succession of drawings two men playing a game of *Tabula*. It is very much like a strip cartoon or comic. The first frame shows the men playing *Tabula* and arguing about how the dice have fallen. The final frame has them squaring up to each other, ready to exchange blows. The owner of the tavern is pushing them out and the caption beneath the painting reads: 'Go outside if you want to fight!'

Gambling became such a craze during the time of the Republic that attempts were made to prohibit or at the very least limit it. It was always permissible to stake money on the outcome of matters of skill such as chariot racing or gladiatorial combat; the objection was to games of chance, those involving dice being the ones particularly frowned on. This legal distinction still exists in Britain today, the law being applied differently to games of skill than to those of chance. A number of high-profile bankruptcies resulted from the gambling of whole estates on a throw of the dice and gambling was thought by some to be harming the moral fibre of the Roman nation. Of course, passing laws is one thing, enforcing them is another matter entirely. Laws theoretically fixed a fine of four times the money staked in the game for those caught gambling on a game like *Tabula* where dice were used. Apart from the days around the feast of Saturnalia, which took place at the same time as our Christmas, gambling on games of chance was forbidden. Just as with the prohibition of alcohol in America during the 1920s, this only had the effect of driving the thing underground.

A number of emperors were devoted to gambling and so in imperial Rome, ordinary citizens tended to take their cue from them. Claudius, for example, was allegedly so addicted to *Tabula* that he had a travelling set devised and attached to his chariot. He also wrote an academic book on the subject of gambling. Commodus, a later emperor, once turned his whole palace into a combined brothel and gambling den.

Huge quantities of gaming pieces made from bone, antler, glass and pottery have been unearthed; not only in London but across the whole of Britain. Wherever the Romans went, they took with them their games of chance. The great advantage of simple board games like *Tabula* is that they require no complicated equipment. One can mark out a *Tabula* board on a tile or off-cut from a wooden plank and the playing pieces themselves can be nothing more sophisticated than pebbles or bits of shaped, sun-dried clay. Dice were often made of bone, although they could also be of carved stone. The numbers were arranged just as they are on modern dice, with those on opposite faces adding up to seven. Because they were not made in factories to precise specifications, most of these dice had a bias towards falling on certain numbers rather than others. The owner of a die would therefore have a slight but distinct advantage when playing a game using his own dice. Knowing what numbers were more likely than others to come up gives one a distinct edge when playing board games of this sort.

In fact, one does not even need dice to play games like *Tabula*. Six flat pebbles, each marked on one side, will do the trick. Just toss them up and count the number which land marked side up. Senet sticks, which have their origin in Egypt, are used in the same way. In this case, flat sticks are used which are coloured on one side.

Latrunculi, also known as *Ludus Latrunculorum*, was another game popular with those in London. Played on a board divided up in the same way as a chess board, *Latrunculi* is a game of strategy, somewhat similar to chess. Once again, the components can be put together from a handful of stones and an old tile or piece of wood.

Apart from board games, dice were used by themselves for gambling. Roman soldiers were famously unable to abstain from playing dice wherever they were stationed. There is mention of this in the Bible. According to Luke's Gospel, while Christ was dying on the cross, the soldiers played dice for his clothes (Luke 23:34).

At Southwark in south London, an exceedingly curious die was found. It is a stone cube with letters instead of numbers engraved upon the faces. Just as with a standard die, the number of letters on opposite faces added up to seven. The letters on the dice were P, VA, EST, ORTI, VRBIS and ITALIA. Some of these groups of letters spelled words: ITALIA means 'Italy' and VRBIS means 'risen'. It has been guessed that several dice of this sort would be cast at once and the challenge would be to spell words or make up sentences from the letters which were on the upturned faces of the dice. Perhaps this was an early version of something akin to 'Scrabble'?

Another game which was widely played needed nothing more complicated that a few copper coins. It was called 'Heads and Ships' and involved tossing coins and trying to predict whether they would land heads or tails. Small denomination Roman coins frequently had a galley on their reverse side, hence the name of this game. Since there are accounts of this game being played by throwing the coins against a wall, the suspicion arises that the old game of 'Pitch and Toss' might well have been played as well. Well within living memory, working-class men in this country played 'Pitch and Toss' with pennies, which entails throwing coins at a wall and trying to ensure that they stay as close to the wall as possible.

Apart from playing games of this sort, how else might those living in Roman London have passed their spare time? Once again, we turn to the recent past to see what sort of things ordinary people did in the evenings and at weekends before there were computers, televisions and mobile phones. Playing musical instruments, singing and reciting were all popular as 'party pieces' at social gatherings. The Celts were great ones for memorising long stories and later reciting them. This is very common in pre-literate societies. One can easily imagine an evening being whiled away in this fashion, with the Romanised Celtic Londoners giving dramatic recitals of the Iron Age equivalent of *The Wreck of the Hesperus*.

Musical instruments have been found from this period in London and the nature of them suggests that these were only for use in domestic settings. In 1989, for instance, a *syrinx* was found during archaeological investigations being conducted on a building site in Upper Thames Street, in the heart of Roman London. The *syrinx* is perhaps better known as panpipes and it is a musical instrument played by blowing across the top of pipes of differing lengths. The one found in London was made of boxwood and was very small – 4½in long and less than 2in wide. A small *syrinx* of this type does not produce a loud tone. Had we uncovered a trombone or kettle drum, it might be possible to hypothesis that it belonged to a commercial venture such as an orchestra, but little panpipes like this are almost certain to be played for amusement in a home or other small-scale setting.

The *syrinx* found at the site in Upper Thames Street could not be dated more accurately by context than between the second and eighth centuries AD, but the design was all but identical with known Roman instruments from the continent, which more or less precludes the one in London being later than the end of the fourth century. The five pipes were tuned to Bb, C, D, E and G. Other examples of panpipes have turned up elsewhere in the country; some made of pottery, others, like the ones from London, made of wood.

Panpipes like this were not fantastically expensive, but nor were they cheap, mass-produced, 'throwaway' items. Most likely, they would be used for musical evenings at home; much as in Victorian times a London family might have gathered round the piano to sing. Before electronic gadgets became all but ubiquitous for both entertainment and communication, this is just the sort of thing that a family might do to entertain themselves for a few hours after the day's work was completed. It is a tradition which has almost vanished in this country, but still lingers on in other, less technologically advanced societies. This is almost certainly one of the ways that Londoners would while away their time in the evening; one person playing the *syrinx* and others singing. It was the Roman equivalent of a mouth organ.

So much for domestic amusements. Living in a Roman city, though, implied communal entertainments as well as those taking place in a purely private capacity. London offered two of the archetypal Roman ways of passing leisure time in the company of others. These were the baths and the amphitheatre. Let us look first at the amphitheatre, which has become a shorthand symbol for one aspect of Roman civilisation: the cruelty and indifference to suffering which was a feature of the gladiatorial combats and other exhibitions to be seen in the arena.

Juvenal referred contemptuously to the desire of the populace for *panem et circenses*, bread and circuses. He used this expression to sum up what he saw as the degeneracy of the times in which he lived, that the ordinary men and women wanted nothing more than cheap food and mindless entertainment of the most debased kind. Intellectuals like Juvenal may well have been right; the shows at amphitheatres tended to cater for the basest instincts. They were, however, enormously popular. Some indication of the popularity of the amphitheatre in London may be seen in by its size.

We do not know the population of London at the time that the amphitheatre was built in the early second century AD. Guesses vary between 20,000 and 30,000. If we take the figure of 20,000 and work with this, then the capacity of the amphitheatre is truly astounding. It has been estimated that 6000 could have been accommodated in the London amphitheatre. This is almost as many as the Albert Hall holds. Six thousand people would represent just under a third of the entire population of the city at that time. A stadium of comparable size in present-day London would need to seat over 2 million people.

That 6000 people out of a total population of 20,000 or 30,000 could fit into the amphitheatre strongly suggests that it was an enormously popular form of entertainment. Before we go any further, we should look at this building in detail and see where it fitted in to the overall scene in Roman London.

It had long been conjectured that an amphitheatre had existed in London, but it was not until some extensive rebuilding around the Guildhall in the City of London during the 1980s that it was found. Fortunately, the parts of the amphitheatre which came to light included the entry gate into the arena. In 1951, a small section of curved Roman wall had been glimpsed during building work which followed bomb damage during the Second World War. The location of this wall, which was clearly part of the wall around the arena, enabled archaeologists to calculate the overall size of the structure.

London's first amphitheatre was constructed in about AD 75. It was little more than a large pit dug in the marshy ground and surrounded with wooden benches. In the early part of the second century, efforts were being made generally to smarten London up and transform it into an entirely Roman city. These efforts roughly coincided with the visit of the emperor Hadrian in AD 122, but whether all the building work was undertaken to spruce things up before his visit or whether he suggested things when he was here is not known.

The amphitheatre was rebuilt in stone, with wooden stands of the sort found in football stadia today. Since it was built on such a grand scale, accommodating perhaps as many as a third of London's citizens, it seems likely that a day at the amphitheatre was a very popular entertainment. The best comparison would be with the regular visits to the cinema made by ordinary workers in this country during the thirties and forties. Because these people spent their time in drab homes and lived dull lives, many of the cinemas at this time made a great effort to be visually impressive. They were built like palaces, so that while they were there, the patrons could feel that they were escaping entirely from their day-to-day lives.

The amphitheatre provided a similar escape from reality for Roman Londoners. As all that remains of such places now is white or grey stone blocks, we sometimes visualise temples and amphitheatres as being fairly anaemic and colourless. Nothing of the sort; these were meant to dazzle the senses. The London amphitheatre had plastered walls, brightly painted. Architectural highlights were picked out in coloured stone and Italian marble. It would have been a breathtakingly exotic sight. Everything about the amphitheatre was exciting and very different from ordinary life. Only a few low sections of wall remain today. In Colour Plate 15, we see a part of what is left. This is part of the curved wall around the arena. Some idea of the scale of this arena may be gained from looking at Colour Plate 13. This shows a photograph of the open space outside the London Guildhall; the curved black line of the left shows where the wall of the arena would have been. It is clear that this would have been a sizable stadium.

What would Roman Londoners have seen at the amphitheatre? The short answer to this is that we do not really know. We are able to extrapolate from what we know of the exhibitions laid on at other similar places and there are also clues to be found in discoveries elsewhere in the city. Mention of amphitheatres and arenas in ancient Rome brings to mind almost at once the image of gladiatorial combats to the death. Is there any direct evidence that such events took place in London? Unfortunately, there is no solid evidence at all, although there are some intriguing indications. Curiously enough, the only real archaeological remains which have been tentatively attributed to a London gladiator are those of a young woman.

Female gladiators were very rare and regarded by jaded audiences as something of a novelty turn. There are a number of references to the practice of women fighting in the arena and it was made the subject of specific laws of the Roman Empire on more than one occasion. In 19 BC, an edict banned the recruitment of the daughters and granddaughters of senators to fight as gladiators. Two hundred years later the emperor Septimus Severus also banned female gladiators, referring to its 'recrudescence among upper class women and the raillery this provokes'. Both these laws mentioned upper class women in connection with gladiatorial combat. Juvenal has something to say about this sort of thing in his Satires. He writes:

These are the girls who blast on the trumpets in honour of Flora.
Or, it may be they have deeper designs, and are really preparing
For the arena itself. How can a woman be decent
Sticking her head in a helmet, denying the sex she was born with?
Manly feats they adore, but they wouldn't want to be men,
Poor weak things (they think), how little they really enjoy it!
What a great honour it is for a husband to see, at an auction
Where his wife's effects are up for sale, belts, shin-guards,
Arm-protectors and plumes!
Hear her grunt and groan as she works at it, parrying, thrusting;
See her neck bent down under the weight of her helmet.
Look at the rolls of bandage and tape, so her legs look like tree-trunks,
Then have a laugh for yourself, after the practice is over,
Armour and weapons put down, and she squats as she used the vessel.
Ah, degenerate girls from the line of our praetors and consuls

'Degenerate girls from the line of our praetors and consuls' hints once again that it was the wealthy and those in the higher social strata who indulged in this activity.

When the grave of a woman in her twenties was being excavated in Southwark in 1996, during the investigation of a Roman graveyard, two things struck those examining it. First, it was clearly that of somebody who was pretty well off. Secondly, the grave lay outside the cemetery, as though the person interred there was some kind of outcasts. There was clearly something a little out of the ordinary about this grave, which lay a stone's throw from Borough tube station. A close look at the grave goods shed some light upon who and what she had been. Although she had been cremated, enough of the pelvis remained uncharred to confirm that this was the skeleton of a woman. Fragments of a lavish funeral feast were also found, indicating that this was no pauper. Eight terracotta bowls were also found in the grave. These had been used for burning cones of the stone pine. The only place in London where stone pines were known to have been growing at that time was near the amphitheatre. The cones were also burned there to mask the smell of death and decay which lingered around such places like an evil miasma. Finally, there were oil lamps, one of which showed a gladiator in action. Taken altogether, staff from the Museum of London concluded that it was more likely than not that the evidence showed this to be the grave of a female gladiator.

We know that gladiatorial combat took place at other amphitheatres in Britain and there is no particular reason to suppose that London would be any different. What else would the audiences have been able to see there? Animal fights very similar to bullfighting would certainly have been on offer. We must remember that cockfighting, bearbaiting and other similar blood sports were still popular with Londoners as late as the nineteenth century. On either side of the entrance into the arena at London have been discovered small cells or waiting rooms. It is supposed that these were to hold animals before they were released for the show.

Another spectacle which Londoners relished for many centuries, again until the nineteenth century, was public execution. There can be no doubt that seeing criminals done to death in various ways would have been an entertaining family day out for Roman Londoners, just as were the hangings at Tyburn some 1500 years later. Again, we have no direct evidence from this, just records of the sort of events which featured at similar places in the province.

There would probably have been religious ceremonies in the amphitheatre as well. London was well provided with temples catering for a wide range of religions and the amphitheatre would make a grand place for a public display. As it was so close to the fort, the suggestion has been made that on the days that public displays were not being staged, the soldiers would use the arena for training. Again, there is no direct evidence for this, but it is quite plausible.

The bathhouse was a Roman institution. When Agricola talked of introducing the Britons to the benefits of the Roman way of life, he must surely have had the regular visit to the bathhouse in mind. According to Tacitus, under Agricola rule the Britons became enamoured of 'the lounge, the bath, the elegant banquet'.

Some grand houses had their own private bathhouse attached to them. This was as rare as having your own indoor swimming pool would be for a modern family. The overwhelming majority of Londoners would have to satisfy themselves with a trip to the public bathhouse. Before we go any further, we must consider one or two important points if we hope fully to make sense of this Roman custom.

First, there were no individual baths for the Romans. Bathing was almost by definition something one did in the company of others. The same was also true, of course, for lavatories, which to us seems extraordinarily odd. Surviving latrines consist of rows of seats side by side so that those opening their bowels could do so while chatting companionably to their neigh-bours. Where private homes had their own bathhouse, there was still no expectation that only one person at a time would be using it. Perhaps this ties in with the very essence of the Roman idea of civilisation; that it meant living cheek by jowl with others in cities. Privacy was in short supply in a Roman city, just as it was in their private homes. We are so used to closing the bathroom door when we have a bath or wish to urinate that all this strikes us as being almost perverted.

Our second point follows on from this. A visit to the baths was about a good deal more than simply removing the dirt from one's body. It was an essentially social occasion, a time to catch up on gossip, meet one's friends and neighbours, conduct business deals, have a snack, do some physical exercises and perhaps even have a snooze. It was like a combined trip to the gym, swimming pool, pub and coffee shop. Making oneself clean because there wasn't a bathtub at home was among the least important aspects of hanging out in the bathhouse.

A number of Roman bathhouses have been discovered in London. The two most notable are those at Cheapside and on Huggin Hill near St Paul's Cathedral. The Huggin Hill baths are among the biggest discovered in this country, although they are fairly small compared with some in Europe. The baths at Cheapside are considerably smaller and it is suspected that they might not have been generally open to the public, but rather designed to serve some special section of the population. They are similar to some known baths attached to army bases and, since they are only a few hundred yards from the fort, it has been thought that they might have been for the exclusive use of the army.

The procedure for a Roman bath was very much like that for a Turkish bath today. There were hot pools, cold pools and space to exercise or just relax and chat. This last was extremely important in London. We know that the city at that time was, as now, a centre of commerce and a place where many financial transactions took place. In Rome, business deals were often clinched during a visit to the baths and there is every reason to suppose that this would also have been the case in London during the same period. Some of the larger baths, like those at Bath in the west, were so big that they could function like swimming pools.

The baths needed plentiful supplies of two things: water and fuel to heat it. Fortunately, there was no shortage of either in London at that time. The forests which encircled the city supplied all the fuel one could wish for and the many streams flowing into the Thames could be diverted to provide water. In Colour Plate 14 we can see an artist's impression of a typical Roman bathhouse. Those at Huggin Hill and Cheapside would have looked very much like this.

Another communal pleasure was just hanging round the forum. This huge public square was full of market stalls and lined on three sides with shops. It was really like a shopping mall, with a covered veranda to protect shoppers from the rain or sun. This was the place to catch up with what was happening in town. There were, of course, no newspapers and so all news travelled by word of mouth. One might conduct a confidential business deal in the baths, but the forum was where one went to hear rumours, scandalous stories and the latest jokes. This was Roman city life. The man who simply stayed at home and minded his own business was not only a dull fellow, he could not really be regarded as civilised at all. Civilised life meant being involved with what was happening in the city and making one's presence known. What better way to do this than strolling round the forum and hearing what was being talked about? In a way, the forum was the heart of the city and a visit there was what living in a city was all about.

7

Religious Beliefs and Practices

The Romans of the early empire had a very easy going and undogmatic approach to religion. Wherever they went, they usually managed to reach an amicable accommodation with the devotees of other faiths, allowing them to flourish alongside their own religion. Often they found similarities between their own ideas and the religions of those whom they conquered, even sacrificing at the temples of other gods themselves. There were two main reasons for this tolerant attitude to other deities. The Roman gods and goddesses were not the original ancestral gods of the Latin people. They had, like so much else in Roman culture, been lifted wholesale from the Greeks. Their names had been changed, but the characters were the same. Jupiter was the chief of the gods and his consort, both wife and sister, was Juno. They were cognate with Zeus and Hera from Greece. These were not omnipotent and benevolent beings that could do no wrong. Rather, they were larger-than-life versions of ordinary, fallible men and women. They were jealous, grew angry, could be spiteful and deceitful; in fact they displayed all the weaknesses of those who worshipped them. The fact that the Roman gods were known to the Greeks by different names showed the Romans that these deities could appear to different nations in various guises. The Greeks knew the goddess of wisdom as Athene, whereas in Italy she went by the name of Minerva. After the annexation of Britain, a goddess of wisdom was encountered who was worshipped by the British at the hot springs of Bath as Sul or Sulis. This was, to the Romans, plainly just another name or perhaps avatar of Minerva. This was one reason why it was so easy for the Romans to combine their gods with those of other parts of Europe. There was another factor.

Roman religion was a matter of contract. One offered sacrifices and the correct devotions to the gods and they rewarded one with victory in battle or prosperity in peacetime. It did not matter whether or not one actually believed in the gods; the important thing was that they were accorded the external honours and devotion to which they evidently thought themselves entitled. That was all that was necessary: outward observance of the proprieties. It was enough to make the sacrifices and offer them prayers. They were pleased with such rituals and would as a matter of course reward those who honoured them in this way. Something else which must be borne in mind is that this traditional religion of Rome declined in importance after the collapse of the Republic in the decades immediately preceding the birth of Christ. The outward observances were maintained, but many Romans did not take their religious practice over seriously. This left the way open during the growth of the empire for the spread of other religions such as the worship of Isis or Mithras. In London, even high-ranking Roman officials were open in their adherence to these heterodox faiths, without anybody in the establishment evidently thinking any the worse of them.

It is true that the Romans suppressed Druidism ruthlessly, but this was because of the political importance of the Druids and their role as a symbol of Celtic resistance to Rome. Once they had been crushed, the Romans had no difficulty acknowledging the Celtic gods and identifying them as avatars of their own deities. The Celtic god Cunomaglos, for example, was accompanied by fierce hounds. Their own Apollo had dogs and so they could readily accept a temple dedicated to Apollo-Cunomaglos. Exactly the same thing happened with Mars, Minerva and Mercury, all of whom were worshipped by both Romans and Britons in so-called Romano-Celtic temples.

There may have been no settlement in the area of London before the Romans, but there are indications that it was some kind of cult centre. Thousands of flints have been dredged from the Thames here, as well as fine examples of bronze weapons and of course many skulls. It seems likely that for thousands of years, people had been coming to that part of the Thames to cast votive offerings into the river. This tradition too continued under the Romans.

We know of a number of Roman temples in London and there is every indication that religion was a pervasive background of everyday life for the inhabitants of the city. It is, of course, quite impossible to know to whether this religious practice was heartfelt or no more than a social convention, rather like respectable people going to church on Sundays in the Victorian age. In addition to the various temples, many homes had *Lares pentares* or household gods – statues and miniature altars to which the householder and his family offered reverence. Most of the temples in Britain were Romano-

Celtic places of worship. This means that they combined the worship of both Celtic and Roman gods, who were often conflated into one personality. They were not classical edifices of white marble, but more modest affairs by far. Some were built on the site of a pre-existing sacred spot; a form either of respect for the local religion or of cultural imperialism, depending upon your point of view. That temples were prominent and well-known places in the city is attested to by the fact that they evidently came to serve as postal addresses. We have a jug from second-century London which is inscribed *Londini ad fanum Isidis* – 'At London, by the Temple of Isis'. It may seem surprising to hear of a temple of Isis in the city, but this is fairly typical of Roman cities. As long as these religions did not provoke their adherents into disobeying Roman edicts and they did not involve disgusting forms of human sacrifice, they were free to worship under Roman rule.

Let us look in detail at some of the temples to be found in London at that time. We shall then examine the role that these places played in the lives of Londoners. In Southwark there are the remains of a temple complex dating from the late first and early second century. It consisted of two square temples set in a courtyard. Also in the courtyard were bases that were probably of altars or cult statues. A nearby stone building, similar to a small villa, has been identified as a guesthouse for worshippers. We know to whom this temple was dedicated because a plaque was discovered on the site which mentions Mars-Camulos. Camulos was the Celtic god of war and so was viewed as being cognate with the Roman god Mars.

Another Romano-Celtic temple has been excavated at Greenwich. The arm of an almost life-size female statue was found there, the hand pierced so that it could hold some rod-like object. It is thought that this object was a bow, making this statue almost certainly one of Diana. A reconstruction of this temple may be seen in Colour Plate 16. It is surrounded by a wall which defines the sacred enclosure around the temple. This was called the *temenos*.

Most Romano-Celtic temples have a similar structure to that shown in the illustration: a small square building, surrounded by a columned veranda. Worshippers did not enter the temple, but gathered in the *temenos* or sacred enclosure, where they made sacrifices or offered up hymns and prayers. Although most were square, some were round or polygonal. The practice was not for communal worship, but individual applications for favours from and sacrifices to the gods.

Why did ordinary people visit temples? At the beginning of the chapter, mention was made of the concept of 'contract' in Roman religion. The Celts would also have been familiar with this idea, even if they did not call it by this name. Across the whole of the Celtic world, including Britain, votive offerings have been recovered from rivers and found buried in the ground. These can be anything from gold jewellery to bronze shields or even ingots of copper. They are gifts to the gods in exchange for their favour. This concept would have dovetailed neatly with the Romans' own ideas about the duties owned to the gods. These temples were not used for collective or communal worship, as churches are almost invariably today. Rather, individuals would visit the temple precinct when they wished to beg a favour or give thanks for some stroke of good fortune. An initial visit might perhaps be made when some enterprise was about to begin. The blessing of the gods would be invoked on some enterprise or a curse made on an enemy. The first visit would often be an exploratory one, in which one sounded out the gods for their reaction to the request being made.

The clearest illustration of how religious practice was observed in London during the Roman occupation may be seen in the so-called 'curse tablets', most of which were made of lead.

Curse tablets were particularly common in Britain, certainly more so than in mainland Europe. They are essentially letters written to the gods and asking them to punish some named person. In return for this, the petitioner would promise to donate money or goods to the temple or sometimes to provide a new altar or undertake building work or repairs to the temple. When the amphitheatre in London was being excavated in the late 1980s, three lead curse tablets were recovered from the arena's drain. One of them was an appeal to the goddess Diana, by a man offering his headgear and scarf, less one third, to deprive of his life the person against whom the curse was directed. This was the first written evidence for the worship of Diana in London, although a stone altar showing Diana was found nearby in the nineteenth century.

Curse tablets of this sort were typically nailed to the walls or columns of temples, hence their Latin name, which is *defixio*. Sometimes, though, they were thrown into rivers or streams; locations which were regarded as borderlines between the real world and the realm of the gods. A number of wax writing tablets have been found in the Walbrook. Judging from its evident importance as a sacred river, it is by no means impossible that these too were thrown into the river as a way of getting a message to the gods. Some cities had a temple quarter and if this was the case in London then the banks of the River Walbrook would have been the logical location.

Religious observance in Roman London would for much of the time have amounted to little more than what we would today call superstition. Digging wells was a ritual act and many of the wells from that period in London have dogs' skulls or even human heads built into their walls. There were certain rites to be followed when digging a well and others to be observed when abandoning a well. When the well was in use, one could always make a minor sacrifice to the gods beneath the earth by dropping things into the well. Such sacrifices ranged from bent pins and broken knives, all the way up to cult statues and stone alters. There was once a Roman well beneath Southwark Cathedral and, when it was excavated in the 1970s, a cult statue about 3ft tall was recovered. This was of a Romano-Celtic hunting god and it was supposed that this had been broken and deposited in the well as a religious ceremony. Another well in central London yielded a statue of the goddess Minerva, again deliberately broken before being deposited.

It is a moot point really, where religion ends and superstition begins. Many people today still touch wood and it is not uncommon to encounter somebody who genuinely believes that ill luck will strike him unless he follows some absurd ritual. Consider the individual who automatically says 'God forbid' when some possible calamity is mentioned. Is this a statement of religious fervour or a superstitious attempt to avert danger? There is a good deal of evidence in Roman London for practices which seem superficially to indicate a devout and god-fearing community, but which on closer examination suggest nothing more than a bunch of people with an elaborate and well-developed system of superstitions.

Across the whole of Europe and large parts of Asia in prehistoric times, rivers, lakes and wells were supposed to have a connection with gods and the world of the dead. Offerings were made to the gods and the spirits of departed ancestors by casting valued possessions into the water. This practice was particularly prevalent in this country. The sort of things sacrificed in this way could be enormously valuable. The great bronze shield fished out of the Thames at Battersea is among the most superb examples of La Tène artwork known in the whole of Europe. It was the equivalent for the warrior who threw it into the Thames a century or so before the Roman invasion to the giving away of a luxury car. This custom lingered on after the establishment of the Roman city of Londinium, but in a very changed form. The offerings made to the spirits of the rivers and lakes in the centuries before the invasion of Britain were often magnificent. Typically, the swords, shields, helmets and spears which were given to the gods in this way were beautifully crafted and almost invariably unused. For a Bronze or Iron Age warrior to abandon such artefacts was truly a sacrifice and suggestive of a high level of religious belief.

Let us now fast-forward a few centuries and see how these sacrificial offerings were conducted in London during the Roman occupation. Things are still being thrown into rivers and wells, but it is immediately apparent that the quality and value of such offerings has declined dramatically. From the Celtic period we have virtuoso pieces of metalwork, spears and swords which have never even been used. What sort of things were the Romans giving to the spirits? Broken tools, worn-out kitchen knives and bent pins. The individuals who chucked this household junk down a well or into the Walbrook or Thames are simply touching wood. They are aware that it is the custom to offer a spear or sword, but cannot see why they should surrender a decent example of these things, which they could use themselves or sell for a profit. The pin symbolises the spearhead as the broken knife does the sword. It is hard to avoid the thought that these people did not really have any reverence or even respect for the spirits to whom they gave these things; they were just going through the motions. This is superstitious ritual rather than religious reverence. We can see this clearly in the discoveries from the period from the Thames, in the vicinity of the bridge leading across the Thames from Cornhill to Southwark.

Many votive offerings have been recovered from the Thames. We looked at some of them above: bronze swords, spears, shields and helmets. Even earlier than these, prehistoric men were depositing worked flints into the river in certain locations. Tens of thousands of these flint weapons and tools were found in the nineteenth century by the Victorians while dredging the riverbed for gravel. These offerings too would have needed a good deal of dedication on the part of those giving them to the spirit of the river; hours of work have gone into some of these pieces. By comparison, what do we find from the Roman period? The commonest finds are low-denomination coins from the middle of the river, right where the Roman bridge once stood. So many have been found that it has been conjectured that a small temple or altar stood in the middle of the bridge and that those passing over threw a penny into the water at this point. Again, this is strongly suggestive of people who are paying lip service to the gods. They have not time to spend hours producing a suitable offering, nor do they wish to give up anything worth keeping. Instead, they will cast a couple of coppers into the river in token respect; much as we might throw a coin into a wishing well.

We return to the idea of the 'contract' in religious practice in Roman London. The first offering was often by way of testing the water, as one might say. Let us suppose that a big favour was being solicited from some specific god. It might be a desire for promotion at work, a wish for an enemy to fall ill, victory in a forthcoming battle; all sorts of things, in fact. The supplicant would visit the temple, altar, sacred well or other place and make a small initial donation. At a temple, this might be some wine or incense, perhaps a cash payment to the priest in charge. The request would then be made in the form of a prayer or petition. A promise would be made, that if the god or goddess' help was forthcoming then the person would provide a new altar or something similar for the temple. The curse tablets at which we looked are examples of this process. Then the petitioner would see what happened. Of course, the god or goddess might not feel inclined to grant the wish. In that case, the libation of wine or pile of incense would simply be written off. It was just one of those things: the gods did not feel able to come across with the goods on this occasion. After all, this was a business proposition which simply fell through. It was a 'no win, no fee' situation. If the gods did not come across with their help, then the supplicant would not provide the new altar or whatever he had pledged for the temple.

If the venture for which the request was made was crowned with success, then an obligation had been incurred to the gods and payment must be promptly and cheerfully made. A number of altars have been found which are inscribed with the name of the person who furnished the temple with them, followed by the letters 'v.s.l.m'. This stands for *Votum solvit lbens merito* – 'willingly performs this vow which was deserved'. Having paid the debt, the business was closed until the next time that a favour was required.

A perfect example of this kind of 'contract' came to light in the London borough of Southwark in 2002, on the site of the Romano-Celtic temple complex which was uncovered during building works. A white, marble plaque was found which had been carefully buried some time in the fourth century. It had originally been fixed to the wall of one of the temples and is interesting for a number of reasons. The inscription reads: 'To the Divine Powers of the Emperors and to the god Mars Camulus, Tiberinius Celerianus, citizen of the Bellovaci, moritix of the people of London first ...' Tantalisingly, the end of the inscription is missing. This is the first inscription that we know of to mention London. Whoever Tiberinius Celerianus was, he clearly had this plaque made and displayed in the temple in order to thank the god Mars-Camulos for something. It is extremely likely that if we could see the whole of this plaque, we should see the letters v.s.l.m. at the bottom.

Apart from the Romano-Celtic temples at which we have looked, there were others dedicated solely to the traditional gods and goddesses of Rome. Although devotion to this state religion waned during the first few centuries of the empire, altars and temples have been found in London that were exclusively for the worship of the Roman deities. In the nineteenth century an altar to Diana was dug up not far from St Paul's Cathedral and this, combined with the lead curse tablet which names Diana mentioned above, has led some to speculate that a temple to this goddess once stood on or near Ludgate Hill. Altars to Jupiter and Juno have also been found.

One of the factors which perhaps damaged the traditional Roman religion was the decision to elevate to the status of gods a number of emperors. We saw that a temple was built and a statue to Claudius was set up in Colchester and the cult of emperor worship was certainly present in London. Now this sort of practice cannot help but have a bad effect upon religion and the way that it is viewed by ordinary people. It is one thing to have some man thousands of years ago who is elevated to the status of god. This is the case with Christianity and even many rational men and women have no real difficulty in accepting that this process might once, under very special circumstances, have taken place. If it is overdone though, this has the effect of, as one might say, 'cheapening the currency'. Romans were invited to believe that a man whom they feasted with and saw getting drunk or consorting with prostitutes might in a few weeks become deified. The more that this happened with emperors, the less that people could take seriously the idea of the gods. Little wonder then that as years went by and more and more divine emperors supposedly joined the pantheon of gods and goddesses, the average citizen grew a little cynical about religion in general. This wholesale assumption of divinity by ordinary men brought the whole concept of religion into disrepute.

There seem to have been a number of temples in Roman London which were devoted to oriental religions without any connection at all to the gods of Rome. The most complete Roman remains relating to religion in London is of course the temple of Mithras, which once stood upon the east bank of the Walbrook. Mithraism was a mystery religion to which only men were allowed admission. It was especially popular with soldiers and merchants. Like Christianity, Mithraism had its roots in the Middle East; specifically in Persia or modern-day Iran. There are connections between this ancient cult and the modern-day Parsees of India and Iran. Mithras was a semi-divine young man whom some have associated with the sun god. He slew a great bull and the animal's blood watered the soil and brought life to vegetation.

It is a debatable point as to whether Mithras was himself a god. There were two main gods in Mithraism: Mazda and Ahriman. Mazda was the good god and Ahriman was his evil adversary. Mithras' role was that of intermediary between men and the gods. There are clear parallels here with Christianity and its own semi-divine young man who acts as a bridge between humanity and the gods. Although Christianity fought against Mithraism and in fact persecuted its followers in London in the later years of the empire, it is not hard to spot great similarities between the two faiths. A visit to the remains of the temple of Mithras in London highlights these common elements.

When it was founded in Iran, the devotees of Mithras worshipped their god-man in caves. As the religion was carried west, most vigorously by the Roman soldiers who adopted it enthusiastically, they built artificial caves; dark, windowless little cellars in which they practised their faith. When London's temple of Mithras was found buried on the bank of the Walbrook in 1954, Londoners queued for hours to view the remains in situ. They were eventually dismantled and rebuilt a few yards away in busy Queen Victoria Street. This was a pity, because the traffic of central London, combined with the raised and exposed site where they are now to be found, are the very antithesis of a Mithraic temple, which should be quiet, dark and subterranean.

Anybody looking at this temple will perhaps feel a jolt of recognition. It may be seen in Colour Plate 17. There is a central nave, lined with pillars. Aisles run alongside these pillars and at the far end of the temple from the entrance is a semi-circular apse. This looks for all the world like a small chapel. There is some reason to suppose that the early Christians actually copied elements from Mithraic temples of this sort and that the general design of our ecclesiastical architecture is in fact based upon temples dedicated to Mithras. Near the apse is an even more familiar element from Christian churches. A square hole shows where a wooden water tank once stood. This was used for the ritual baptism of initiates to the cult, precisely as the font in a church is used today.

For some while, Mithraism was practically the state religion of the Roman Empire. We tend to think of the pantheon of gods about whom we learned at school as being the official religion of ancient Rome, but these gods and goddesses faded a little in importance after the end of the Republic. This might go some way to explain how easy the Romans found it to accommodate Celtic and other gods whom they encountered and why they did not worry overmuch about worshipping these alongside their own traditional deities. The emperor Commodus was initiated into the Mithraic religion at the end of the second century and in the third century the emperor Aurelian proclaimed the worship of 'the unconquered sun' to be the official religion of the entire empire.

The temple in London was built about AD 240. We do not know exactly what went on in these places, although what little we do know indicates a number of other intriguing comparisons with Christianity, quite apart from the architectural design. At one time, it was thought that initiation into the cult of Mithras entailed the sacrifice of a bull and the washing of the new member in the blood of the bull. This is likely to be a scandalous libel perpetrated by the early Christians who detested this energetic religion, so close to their own in many ways. A tank of water stood in the Mithreum when it was in use and it may be that new recruits to the religion were actually washed or even submerged in the water in this tank. This is eerily reminiscent of the Christian rite of baptism. The talk of the blood of the bull was almost certainly symbolic rather than actual. It must be remembered that in Christian churches today, extensive mention is made during the service of Eucharist or communion to 'the blood of the lamb'. This is not say that churches on a Sunday morning are actually awash with blood from a slaughtered lamb. The high point of the Communion is reached when the priest holds up a chalice and claims to the congregation that 'This is the blood of Christ'. It is of course nothing of the sort; merely wine.

The worshippers of Mithras also had a ritual meal of this kind which must have been somewhat similar to the Communion which Christians celebrate today. Not only that, but they celebrated the birth of their god on 25 December. All this, combined with Mithras' role as intermediary and redeemer of mankind, makes it similar enough to Christianity to see why the Christians were determined to stamp it out as soon as they had the power to do so. At some time in the fourth century, the temple of Mithras was rededicated to other, more conventional, Roman gods. Images of Bacchus, Minerva and Mercury were found buried near the temple.

There is reason to believe that the temple was attacked by Christians at some stage and the sacred sculptures which once decorated it were buried to conceal them from a Christian mob. As they themselves worshipped a semi-divine man who had died and risen again, the Christians regarded cults like Mithraism as being especially dangerous for their own faith. Among the sculptures buried at this time was the central image of Mithraism: the Tauroctony. This was a detailed scene of the central act of redemption in Mithraism: the slaying of the bull by Mithras.

We shall look at two other eastern religions before we turn to the evidence for Christianity in London at this time. We saw that a flagon or jug was found which used the temple of Isis as an address. Although we have no idea where this temple was situated, another reference to it was found some years ago. When the riverside wall was being built as protection from Saxon pirates, old chunks of masonry were utilised from tombstones, as well as stones from a monumental arch which once stood near Blackfriars. According to the inscription on a piece of stone used for building the wall, the temple of Isis in London collapsed because it was so old. The governor of Britain at the time, Martiannius Pulcher, apparently ordered it to be rebuilt. This was in the third century. Isis was, like Juno, another Queen of Heaven. Her husband was killed and rose from the dead.

Many items of religious or ritual significance have been fished out of the River Thames. One of these suggests the cult of Cybele and Atys was active in London during the Roman occupation. A pair of bronze castrating forceps was found, which featured the heads of both Cybele and Atys. According to the mythology, Atys castrated himself for the love of Cybele and there are accounts of her worshippers performing this mutilation upon themselves in the goddess' honour. Forceps such as these would have been used both to remove the testicles and also to staunch the flow of blood. Atys was another of those gods who incurred particular disapprobation from the early Christians, because he too, just like their Jesus, died and rose again from the dead. He is usually portrayed like Mithras, wearing a Phrygian cap with the point turned forwards and a couple of statues of Atys have turned up in London. The cult figure recovered from the well beneath Southwark Cathedral appears to be wearing a Phrygian cap and the suggestion has been made that rather than being a British hunter god, this is in fact a representation of Atys.

In the third and fourth centuries there was something of a religious revival in London. This may have been connected with the uncertain times through which people were living. Anxious times often precipitate increased religious observance as people sometimes believe that the attacks by enemies, poor harvests and so on are a punishment from the gods because they have not been sufficiently honoured. Whatever the explanation, there was a revival in the old religion of Rome, which became important again for many citizens in the capital. There was also a resurgence of interest in cults like that of Mithras.

At about this time too, Christianity made itself felt in London. The early evidence for this religion in London is scanty; one might almost say all but non-existent. The first British Christian martyr was of course St Alban, a Roman soldier who sheltered a fugitive cleric and was beheaded some time in the third century. Just when he was executed is a debatable point. Anglo-Saxon sources such as the Venerable Bede cite the year AD 283, while recent work by an his-

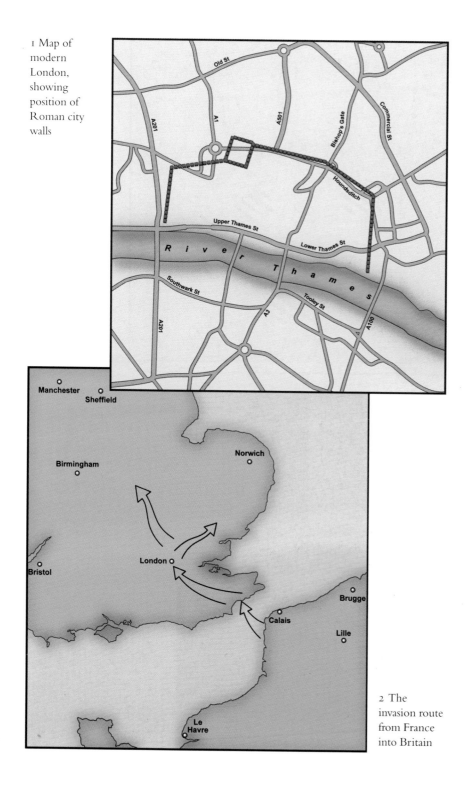

1 Map of modern London, showing position of Roman city walls

2 The invasion route from France into Britain

3 The hills of central
London

4 A Roman marching camp

5 A mud brick made from
London earth

6 The construction of a wattle-and-daub wall

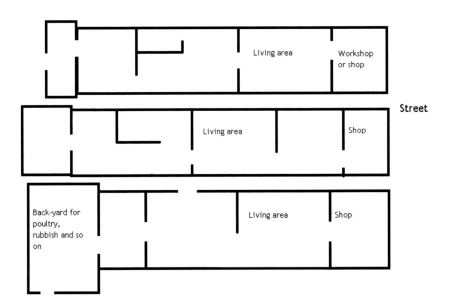

Living area

Workshop
or shop

Street

Living area

Shop

Back-yard for
poultry,
rubbish and so
on

Living area

Shop

7 Plan of typical shops in pre–Boudican London

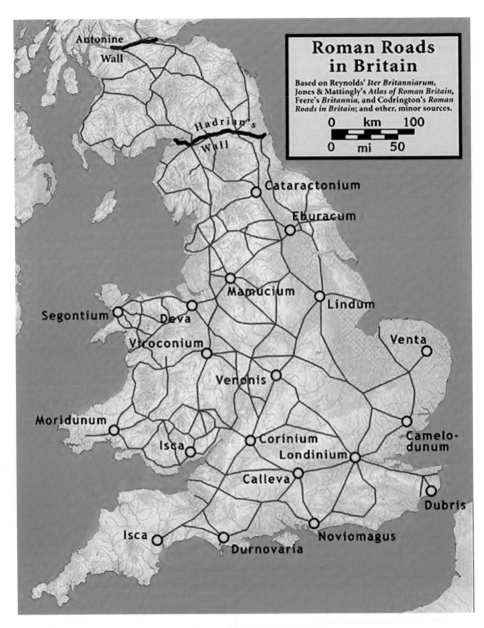

8 The Roman roads of Britain. (Kind permission of Notuncurious, Wikimedia Commons)

9 Domestic floor of red tesserae

10 *Opus signum* flooring

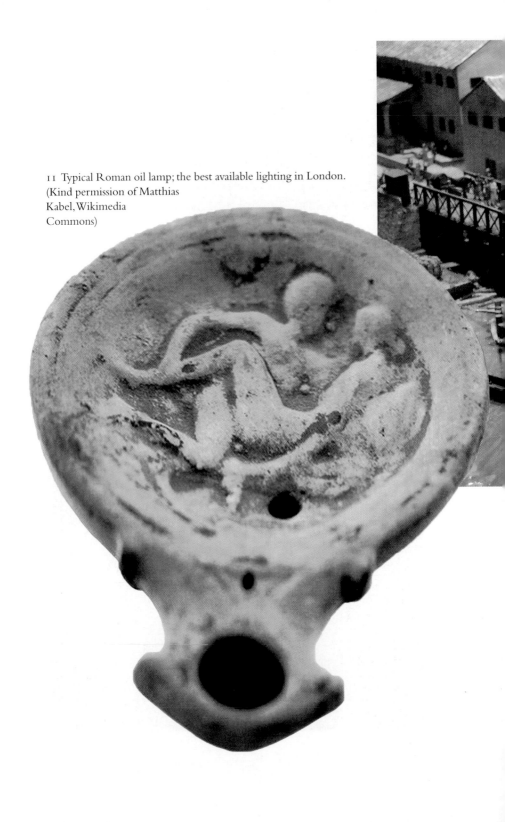

11 Typical Roman oil lamp; the best available lighting in London. (Kind permission of Matthias Kabel, Wikimedia Commons)

12 How Roman London's bridge and docks might have looked. (Kind Permission of Steven G. Johnson, Wikimedia Commons)

13 The site of the amphitheatre today, showing the extent of the arena

14 How a bathhouse in Roman London might have looked. (Kind permission of
www.cyark.org, Wikimedia Commons)

15 Part of the arena wall of the amphitheatre today

17a & 17b The temple of Mithras today

16 How the Romano-Celtic temple at Greenwich looked. (Kind Permission of *Time Team*, Channel 4)

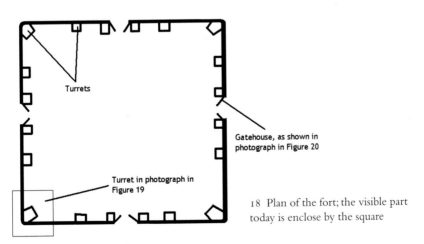

Turrets

Gatehouse, as shown in photograph in Figure 20

Turret in photograph in Figure 19

18 Plan of the fort; the visible part today is enclose by the square

19 The foundation of a corner turret of the fort

20 The west gateway of the fort today

21 The Roman wall at Tower Hill

22 The wall today; still an impressive structure 2000 years later

23 Vertical section of the fort wall (left side) strengthened by the later city wall (right side)

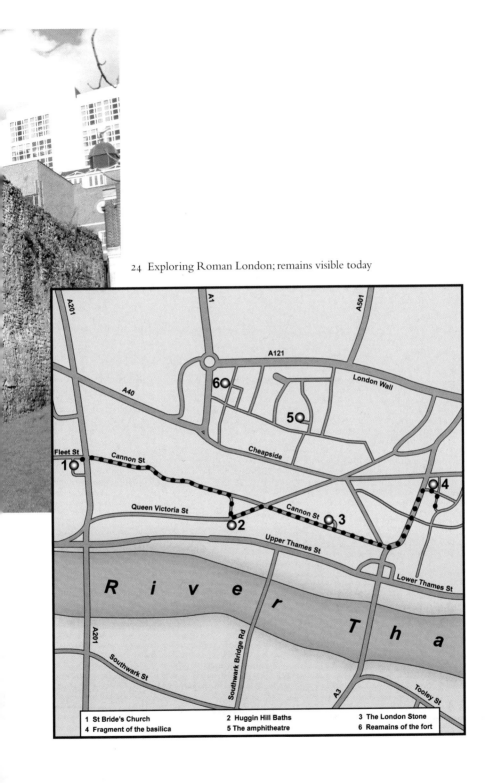

1 St Bride's Church 2 Huggin Hill Baths 3 The London Stone
4 Fragment of the basilica 5 The amphitheatre 6 Reamains of the fort

25 The statue of a hunter god recovered in 1977 from the well beneath Southwark Cathedral (with kind permission of Southwark Cathedral)

torian could put the event as early as AD 209. At any rate, we may be sure that Christianity was present in Britain and being persecuted in the third century.

We also know that in AD 313 the Edict of Milan removed any penalties against Christians for pursuing their faith. The following year, a bishop of London attended the Council of Arles, along with the bishop of York. From then on Christianity was decidedly in the ascendant in London. The sculptures and holy objects from the temple of Mithras were buried in order to protect them from Christian attack in the fourth century and although in the early fourth century the temple was rededicated to Bacchus, it is clear that the Christians were harrying the followers of other faiths and trying to make their own the only religion observed in the city.

In 2006, archaeological investigations beneath St Martins in the Field church in Westminster brought to light a Roman sarcophagus which had been buried along an east–west alignment. This is strongly indicative that it was a Christian burial, but it has not been possible to pinpoint the date other than to be fairly confident that it was from the fourth century. The earliest definite remains of any church in London are those of All Hallows by the Tower: a Saxon wall and archway dating from around AD 750. Not far from All Hallows, a large Roman building from about AD 350 was found in 1993. Not all of it was excavated, but it was claimed that the floor plan was very similar to the Cathedral of St Tecla in Milan. If this is true, then this would make it the earliest church in Britain.

In other words, we can be sure that Christians were living and worshipping openly in London from the early fourth century onwards. When did Christianity actually arrive in London though? Lead ingots have been brought up from a Roman shipwreck in the Thames. They are stamped with the *chi rho*, a Christian symbol made up of the first two letters of Christ's name in Greek. They also bear the inscription *Spes in Deo*: 'Hope in God'. It is impossible to date these ingots precisely, but they are presumed to date from after the Edict of Milan and the official state toleration of Christianity.

More uncertain is the age of a small pewter bowl found in the River Walbrook. It too has the symbol of the *chi rho* scratched on its base. This bowl may be part of a set of liturgical vessels dating from the time when Christianity was prohibited.

In short, it is possible to be sure that Christianity was active in London during the fourth century, but that there is no solid evidence that it was being practised any earlier than this.

8

The Roman Army in London

We saw in Chapter 1 that the first permanent settlement in the area which would later become London was an army marching camp established on Cornhill, a quarter of a mile north of the Thames. Archaeological investigation of this camp shows that it was dismantled shortly after having been built. This was because the invading forces of Claudius' army moved north and west, intending to subdue the rest of the country and it made no sense to leave thousands of troops sitting idly by the river while there was fighting to be done in the north of Britain.

When the Boudican revolt broke out in AD 60, the colony in Colchester appealed to the procurator in London for help and he responded by sending only 200 lightly armed auxiliaries. It is a fair guess that a large body of troops was not at this time stationed in London. Some cities were founded as military bases or garrison towns, but there is no evidence at all to suggest that London was one of them. What we do know is that in the immediate aftermath of the city's destruction by fire, the army moved in and helped with the reconstruction. A military base was built between Cornhill and the Thames and it remained in operation there for about a quarter of a century. One priority was the rebuilding of the jetties and quays which had been burnt.

The new docks for London, which were built after the city's destruction by Boudica, were very well constructed and seemed to have been put together all of a piece very soon after the city was rebuilt. This argues against their being a product of private enterprise and in favour of their having been organised by central authority. Some of the work entailed would have needed heavy-lifting gear; the sort of equipment that army engineers would have ready at their disposal.

Looking at remains from the past and trying to deduce their meaning is a hazardous and uncertain undertaking. We look at a fortification like Hadrian's Wall or the wall around London and assume at once that the purpose of these structures was defensive; they were built to protect people against an armed attacker. In Chapter 10, we shall see that this was not necessarily the case. People reinforce frontiers and erect high walls for all kinds of reasons, many of which have nothing at all to do with defence.

The fort in London, the remains of which may still be seen, was of the classic, so-called 'playing card' design. This expression was coined because the corners of such forts were rounded rather than being sharp angles. Some of these forts are rectangular, while others, like the one in London, are almost square. Colour Plate 18 shows the walls and fortifications of the fort. A tall stone wall had small turrets at the corners and between the corners and the four gateways. One corner of this plan is enclosed by a square. This delineates a part of the fort which can still be seen today; it is described more fully in a later chapter.

London's fort covered an area of about 12 acres. Its walls were built of Kentish ragstone, a type of sandstone, and turrets stood at the corners and also at intervals along the walls. Colour Plate 19 is a photograph of the base of one of the turrets at the south-west corner of the fort. The curvature of the wall can clearly be seen. In the middle of each wall, midway between the corners, were gates. One still remains and a photograph of what can now be seen of it is found in Colour Plate 20. Why was this fort built here? The obvious explanation is that it was here to defend London. After the sack of the city by Boudica's forces in AD 60, it surely made sense to have a military presence in the city – troops who could be called on when need arose. This explanation is simple, clear-cut and easily understandable. Unfortunately, as is so often the case with simple, clear-cut and easily understandable explanations, it is probably quite wrong. The fort in London, although built to the same basic pattern as those in areas where defence was a priority, actually housed clerical workers and civil servants. These workers belonged to the army but were concerned more with administrative duties than fighting.

When we lack clear records and a definitive timeline, we have to make intelligent guesses about just when and why things happened in the past. We know that the fort in London was built round about the same time as the stone amphitheatre and that both these events and quite a bit of other building in stone took place at about the time that the emperor Hadrian visited

Britain in AD 122. For many years, the accepted chronology was as follows. Before Hadrian's visit, London was spruced up and a lot of rebuilding in stone was undertaken. The old wood and turf amphitheatre was replaced with one made of stone and various other civic buildings were similarly rebuilt. During his visit, Hadrian initiated the building of the famous wall which bears his name and then he left. If only history really followed a simple linear narrative in this way!

The above account is satisfying to twenty-first-century readers because they can relate to it. Imagine if the queen was due to visit a town and spend some weeks or months there. Wouldn't they make a great effort to tidy the place up, give it a lick of paint and make it look more presentable? We feel that we can understand the motives of those involved and make sense of history. The only difficulty is that Hadrian's Wall was probably planned and quite possibly actually in the process of being built before Hadrian even set foot in the country. It is also quite as likely that the extensive programme of rebuilding in stone, of which the fort was a part, was instigated by Hadrian himself after a tour of inspection. In other words, in our eagerness to impose our own neat narrative on history, we might have muddled up cause and effect and made a complete nonsense of the whole sequence of the history of that time.

There are a number of clues to the function of the soldiers stationed in London during the second century AD, when the fort in London was operating. The earliest depiction of a Londoner is that provided by a sculpted relief of a soldier, which was found on a Roman tombstone from Camomile Street in the City of London. In his left hand, this legionary is holding six wax writing tablets and a scroll. We know from similar tombstones elsewhere that this was meant to show that this man worked as a clerk. During the second century, the governor in London needed no heavily armed soldiers around him, but rather literate and educated men who could oversee the running of his civil service. Some of the men stationed in the fort would have been his personal bodyguard, but there was little threat of trouble in London after the Boudican revolt and the role of personal guards would almost certainly have been a purely ceremonial one.

One of the greatest puzzles about the Roman fort in London is that it operated for less than a hundred years. By the end of the second century, the fort was no longer being used as a military base. Since this was at a time when the governor of Britain was challenging the Emperor of Rome and launching a civil war to try to seize control of the entire empire, it is hard to see why at this moment the fort should be abandoned as a military fortification, but there it is.

Considering the huge importance of the military during the Roman Empire, it is strange that there is not more evidence of their activity in London. After all, on more than one occasion, governors of Britain declared themselves to be the rightful emperor and took their armies to the continent to launch civil wars against rival claimants to the throne. These troops must have taken ship in London to sail to Europe and one would have supposed that there would have been bases and barracks to accommodate them when they arrived in London. If such facilities did exist, they have yet to be found. Having said that, excavations near the site of the medieval Winchester Place in Southwark did point to the possible existence there of a naval headquarters.

Beneath the ruins of the Bishop of Winchester's Palace in Southwark, on the south side of the Thames, has been found a Roman building with a hypocaust and bathhouse attached to it. Fragments of a marble plaque which appears to list the legions in Britain were found nearby and this has led some to suppose that this might actually have been the headquarters of the army for the entire province. Others have suggested that it might rather have been the offices of the Roman fleet. That this place had some military connection is undeniable, but until further evidence emerges, that is about all that we can say.

We can be confident that troops were based in London after the abandonment of the fort at the end of the second century, but where they lived is unknown. At various times of crisis there must have been large numbers of soldiers in the capital, either waiting to take ship to join in and support the bids for power of British leaders or being stationed permanently in London. In the fourth century, for instance, semi-circular bastions were built on the east wall of London. These held platforms for gigantic crossbows – the catapults. Obviously, defences of this sort would need specialised troops and engineers to maintain them, but we have no idea at all where they would have been living.

It may be that in the future new evidence will emerge about the military history of London during the Roman period. For now, all we can say with confidence is that marching camps with earth ramparts were built at least twice in the first century and that for 80 years after that a stone fort was used by soldiers. Anything much beyond this takes us into the realm of educated guesswork.

9

The City in Decline

In Chapter 4 we saw Roman London reach its zenith. The emperor Hadrian visited the city in AD 122 and many buildings were refashioned either before or after his stay. Londoninium had a stone amphitheatre, large public baths, an impressive palace for the governor, a fort; all the trappings of an important Roman city. There seemed no limit at all as to how large and prosperous the city could become and after Hadrian had returned to Rome; it is reasonable to assume that the citizens of London were feeling pretty pleased with themselves and proud of their city. Nobody could possibly have guessed that within a few years, London would begin to dwindle and its population decline until there was no need for many of these fine facilities.

A couple of years after the visit of Hadrian, London was devastated by a fire or perhaps series of fires. No mention is made of these fires in any of the writings of that time and so we are compelled to rely upon the archaeological record. This consists of another 'red layer', overlaying that resulting from Boudica's destruction of the city 60 or 70 years earlier. All the indications are that this fire or fires destroyed a greater area than was affected when Boudica's followers torched the whole city. It looks as though a large part of London was burnt to the ground in about AD 125. We do not know of any sort of fighting or rebellion at this time and so it must be assumed that any fire was accidental. We must remember that despite the building of a few palaces and bathhouses in stone, the majority of the population still lived in house made of wood or wattle-and-daub. Many of these had thatched roofs. These highly combustible buildings were all crammed together and once one went up, many would inevitably also burn.

In Rome itself, fire was a constant background anxiety. Despite having no fewer than seven fire brigades in the city, fires were a commonplace occurrence. It could hardly have been otherwise with all lighting being provided by open flames. In Rome and other cities of the empire, laws were passed which theoretically compelled householders to extinguish their fires at a certain hour, but such ordinances were widely ignored. After all, in the winter, the fire in the hearth was the only source of warmth in the entire house. In London, a far colder place than Rome, this would have been even more the case. Given a choice between worrying about the risk of the house catching fire on a bitterly cold winter's night and the children freezing to death, most families opted to keep the fire burning. With this situation prevailing in thousands of wooden buildings, house fires were an inevitable hazard and frequent occurrence.

There is no indication that the second destruction of the city by fire had any particular effect upon its development and growth. The citizens rebuilt their homes and by the middle of the second century there were more inhabitants than ever; perhaps as many as 50,000 people were living in the city at this time. The seeds for London's decline lay not in the burning of its houses; as was seen after Boudica's attacks, a vibrant and healthy community can cope with this sort of misfortune. There were actually two factors which would halt the expansion of the city and cause it to contract in on itself, changing from an energetic, thrusting powerhouse into a stagnating backwater. Hadrian had unwittingly sown the seeds for this process during his stay in AD 122.

One of the things that the emperor Hadrian was keen to do was to mark the limits of the empire. This was to be done by establishing clear and distinct borders along the edges of the empire. In some areas, northern Europe and north Africa for instance, natural physical boundaries already existed which served to delineate the Roman Empire form the barbarian world. The River Rhine in Germany was one such natural border and the Sahara desert was another. Elsewhere, roads and wooden fences were laid out, so that those on both sides of the border knew the position.

Now it will also be remembered that during the time of the Republic, limits were set upon colonisation; it was to be restricted to the lands which bordered the Mediterranean, the known world. Merchants and traders were not content with edicts of this sort. They needed new territories in order to thrive; new markets for their goods; and unknown lands which could be exploited for their natural resources. The annexation of Britain was a welcome move from a purely economic viewpoint for this class. Hadrian had now firmly indicated by the establishment of physical borders that the expansion of the empire was at an end. No new markets, no more areas to be investigated for the raw materials which they might provide. What you see is what there is.

In the province of Britannia, this mentality was represented physically by the building of a wall: Hadrian's Wall, which stretched from the shore of the Irish Sea in the west to the North Sea in the east. Whatever its defensive purpose, which was dubious at best, this great wall certainly had the effect of cutting off Scotland from the province of Britannia. At one time, the next logical step in the westward expansion of Roman influence had been the eventual invasion and occupation of Ireland and Scotland. This long-term aim had now been officially abandoned. It might be mentioned that most of the gold in the British Isles, to mention just one raw material of great interest to the Romans, lay not in England and Wales, but in Scotland and Ireland. These areas were now effectively cut off from further exploration and economic exploitation.

What did all this have to do with London? London has, from its earliest days as a Roman province, always been a place for trading and exchange. This tradition has continued down the ages and is still the defining characteristic of that part of London which was once the city of Londinium. The City of London, the area enclosed by the Roman wall, is synonymous with finance and trade. Talk today of 'the City' and everybody knows that you are referring to financial affairs. With half the British Isles now effectively closed to further exploration and trade, the importance of London inevitably dwindled. Those already working in the City had by now all the contacts with local areas tied up and there was little scope for newcomers to carve out new business empires or franchises for themselves. The impetus which had led so many chancers and carpetbaggers to descend upon the city in its early days had now evaporated. Had Ireland been opened up to trade, then there would doubtless have been a gold rush, as adventurers from the continent flooded into London to take advantage of these new opportunities. However, it was not to be and those seeking new business now looked more to the east than to the west of the empire which, with the building of Hadrian's famous wall, had become both physically and commercially a dead end.

The closing down of commercial opportunities in this way might not have been enough in itself to precipitate a decline in London's fortunes. The effect of anything of this sort would in any case be gradual. It was not that businessmen were leaving London; rather that new ones were not flocking there. The overall effect should have been a slower rate of growth, both of the population and the area of the city which was inhabited. At most, this would result in stagnation and no further growth at all. Another factor came into play in the second half of the second century which caused a dramatic change in London's prospects.

From AD 165 until about 180, Europe was swept by a mysterious illness. Known either as the Antonine Plague, after the family name of Marcus Aurelieus, the emperor at that time, or alternatively as the Plague of Galen, a famous Roman physician, the effects of this virulent disease were disastrous for the empire. Estimates of the death toll vary, but it is believed that around 5 million people died altogether in the course of the plague. Places like legionary barracks were ideal for the spread of a contagious disease and in some garrison towns the army was decimated. This led to serious problems with maintaining the borders of the empire. In Germany, for example, Marcus Aurelius had great difficulty in mustering enough troops to drive back barbarian incursions from across the Rhine.

It has been suggested that the mortality rate of the Antonine Plague was between 10 per cent and 25 per cent. Many authors pinpoint this time as the beginning of the decline of the Roman Empire, a decline which was, as we shall see, mirrored in Roman London. What was this dreaded illness which wreaked such havoc across the whole of the empire? Until quite recently, it was thought that the Antonine Plague was either smallpox or measles. Molecular biology now indicates that measles did not emerge as a separate illness until around AD 500, which means that it could not have been implicated as a factor in the Antonine Plague. This leaves smallpox as the sole remaining suspect and it is this exceedingly infectious disease which most modern experts assume to have been at work. The symptoms certainly fit: the pustules, fever and diarrhoea are all in keeping with a diagnosis of smallpox. Galen wrote extensively about treating victims of this plague, but his work was purely pragmatic. He was concerned with treating the disease, not providing a textbook for future medical historians.

The Antonine Plague swept across Gaul and Germany. Although there are no historical records, it is inconceivable that Britain should have escaped its ravages. It would have struck first in London and spread out from there to the rest of the country. London was the foremost port of the province and the infection would have been brought here by travellers on board ships from Gaul. The crowded conditions of Roman London, with 50,000 people crammed into a space of only a few hundred acres, would be ideal for the spread of a virulently contagious disease of this sort. Sanitation was still primitive, with human faeces still being dumped near wells and streams where families fetched their drinking water. It must have raged through the city like a fire. Small wonder that the population of the city apparently plummeted in the final years of the century.

There may be no direct record of the Antonine Plague in London, but indirect evidence for a sudden drop in the city's population is everywhere. In the first half of the second century, Roman London was sprawling across both sides of the Walbrook, from the future location of the Tower of London in the east, all the way to Fleet Street in the west. The River Fleet made a natural boundary to the city's expansion, but Ludgate Hill and the area between the Barbican in the north and the Thames in the south was crowded with workshops and residential districts. By AD 200, the area west of the Walbrook had been abandoned. The houses and workshops had been deliberately demolished and rich black earth had been brought in from outside the city, presumably with the intention of gardening or farming. The same thing happened across the river in Southwark and, to a lesser extent, in the rest of the city. At the same time, the large public bathhouse on Huggin Hill was demolished. This was perhaps because the expense of running such an establishment could no longer be justified by the smaller population.

That housing and shops in parts of the city were being knocked down and replaced by fertile soil brought in from the countryside suggests strongly that some residents at least were trying to combine city dwelling with a more rural lifestyle. The only possible reason for wanting this earth must have been to grow things. The soil in central London is yellow and mixed with a lot of clay. In the summer it bakes hard as rock and in the winter becomes greasy and slimy. It is terrible for agriculture. What sort of things were people hoping to grow in this way? There are several possibilities.

We can probably discount the idea that these were individual gardens where flowers were being grown. Perhaps this was part of some new enterprise, market gardening to provide fresh vegetable for those living in London? This is quite possible. Or, in view of the political developments at which we shall look in a moment, there might have been a government-inspired campaign to promote self-sufficiency and reduce dependence upon imported food. Something akin to the 'dig for victory' campaign in this country during the Second World War. By that reading of the situation, the governor of London would have ordered the demolition of empty homes between the Walbrook and the Fleet and arranged for earth to be dumped there. This part of London would then have been divided up into allotments where families could grow their own vegetables. Before we look at the circumstances which might have brought about such a project, there is one final change in the use of various parts of second-century London at which we must look.

Some time around the end of the first century AD, a stone-built fort went up in London. It covered an area of 12 acres and was home to perhaps a thousand men. Most of these soldiers were probably civil servants and administrators rather than fighting men, while others may have had guard duties or purely ceremonial roles. At any rate, it was a useful thing to have in the capital city, especially in view of the upheavals at which we are about to look. Nevertheless, by the end of the second century, less than a hundred years after it had been built, this fort was no longer being used for any military purpose.

We have seen that one of Claudius' motives in invading Britain and stationing troops in the country was to prevent any military commander in Europe from building up too large an army and using it to further his political ambitions. This is, of course, just what Julius Caesar did when he crossed the Rubicon and marched on Rome. By moving 40,000 soldiers or so to Britain, it would prevent a large army building up on the German border, say. Ever since the last days of the Republic, military force had been the key to success when trying to secure the coveted role of emperor. No emperor could hope to survive for long without the backing of the army, or at least a larger part of it than any rival could command.

On the last day of AD 192, the emperor Commodus was assassinated in Rome. The throne then went to Helvius Pertinax, who was himself murdered three months later. There was no clear line of succession and so it looked as though whoever could gain the backing of the greatest part of the army would get the post of emperor. Three main claimants emerged. One of these was the governor of Britain, a nobleman called Clodius Albinus. The other two were also provincial governors. Septimus Severus commanded forces on the Rhine and Danube, while in Syria was

Prescenius Niger. It was a question of who had the greatest number of loyal troops at his command.

Clodius Albinus had three legions in Britain and one in Spain; Niger had nine in the Middle East; but Severus had 16 legions in total who owed him their personal allegiance, and he marched on Rome to enforce his claim to the throne. Not wishing to find himself fighting a war on two fronts, he made a deal with Clodius Albinus, whereby the succession would pass to him on Severus' death. Having thus bought himself time with one dangerous rival, he moved east and defeated Prescenius Niger. At this point, the governor of Britain felt that it was worth contesting the point and took his own armies across the Channel to challenge Severus for the throne. We have looked in some detail at this power struggle because the outcome had both profound implications for London and also set an unfortunate precedent for the future behaviour of governors of this country in the following centuries.

10

A Walled City

We have seen the small trading post of London grow to be the capital of the province of Britannia. It became a mighty city, visited by the emperor Hadrian, with bathhouses and impressive public buildings, including a basilica, forum, fort and amphitheatre. We then watched as London declined somewhat, the population shrinking and some built-up areas of the city being transformed into allotments and vegetable gardens. The bathhouses were demolished, as were many of the buildings in the Walbrook valley, particularly on the west side. It is strange and at first more than a little puzzling that it should have been at this stage, when the city was plainly past its peak, that the decision should have been made to construct a gigantic city wall enclosing not only the main buildings of the city, including the fort and amphitheatre, but also a lot of cultivated fields, as well as grassland which never had been built upon and never would be.

Perhaps we should pause at this point and ask ourselves why the Romans built some other high walls like that which separated the Roman province of Britain from the wild land of Caledonia, modern-day Scotland. It is by looking at this latter wall, which we know today as Hadrian's Wall, that we might find a clue as to the reason for undertaking the enormous task of enclosing almost 350 acres of the Thames valley with a stone wall. Make no mistake about it, this was a massive project. London's wall was 2 miles long, 20ft high and 8ft thick. It needed over a million blocks of Kentish ragstone, all of which had to be brought by boat from quarries near Maidstone in Kent.

Before we look in detail at the physical challenge of building a great wall of this sort, I want to think a little about the possible purpose of such a barrier. Why build it in the first place? On the face of it, this seems an absurd question. Why do people build high, stone walls? Obviously as a defence of some sort; to keep somebody out. Walls can certainly keep enemies out and this is probably what of most of us instinctively assume when we think about a wall like that which was erected around London; it was to prevent armed men from storming the city. This is pretty much what used to be thought about Hadrian's Wall as well; it was there to prevent attacks from those on the other side of the wall. Obvious, when you think about it. Walls like that protect people from those who would do them harm. It is no different in principle from a high wall around our house and garden; it stops trespassers and burglars entering our property.

Of course, walls like that on the Scottish border or the one which encircled London keep out other things besides armed men. All sorts of items being brought into the province from Scotland would have to pass through one of the gates in Hadrian's Wall. This might include anything from gold to herds of sheep. Goods being exported will also have to go through a gate under the control of the military. The same applies to a port like London. Produce being sent to the continent from Britain would, before reaching the docks, have to enter London via one of the gates in the wall. Goods brought into London by sea would similarly have to be carried through these same gates before they could reach another part of the country. People travelling to and from Britain would have to pass regularly through the same gates.

We will return to this point shortly, but first it is necessary to look a little at the background against which the building of London's wall took place. At the end of the second century AD, a power struggle took place in Rome as to who should become the next emperor. This was won by Septimus Severus, who had the backing of some of the legions in Europe. While he was consolidating his position, the governor of Britain took the opportunity to declare himself emperor and crossed the Channel with his own army to try to seize the throne by military force. His attempt failed and he ended up committing suicide following his defeat in battle in AD 197.

Since this brief civil war took place roughly when the London wall was built, it was for a long time assumed that there was some connection between the two events. Perhaps before he sailed for Europe, the governor had decided to fortify his capital and protect it against a counter-attack from the forces of Severus. There are several difficulties with this hypothesis.

The trickiest problem with the idea of London's wall as a hastily thrown-up defence erected in the course of a brief struggle for supremacy is that such a massive and well-made structure could not possibly have been built in a hurry. It would have taken at least two years to complete. We know this because we have records of the buildings of castles and city walls in the medieval period. As a rule of thumb, a castle would increase in height by 10ft a year. We have an example of a wall which was built in a hurry to protect London from enemies during the Roman period and this is the river wall which was put in place around 150 years after the main wall. This shows every sign of having been done in a hurry. It uses various materials; in places there are no foundations; old tombstones are simply stuck straight into the clay of the river bank. The riverside wall is an awful bit of work: wood, clay, lumps of chalk, bits of masonry from a monumental arch; anything that came to hand. This was most definitely a wall that was patched together as a rushed job in response to an emergency and it shows.

London wall shows none of this haste. It was a carefully planned enterprise built to the highest specifications. The stone was quarried in Kent and brought up the River Medway and along the Thames. The foundations are secure, layers of tile are incorporated every few feet to endure that the courses are level. The sections which have not been deliberately demolished are as solid now as they were almost 2000 years ago; this was not some jerry-built defensive work cobbled together in a mad rush because the governor wanted to nip off to the continent next month to start a civil war. It is a perfectly planned and executed piece of civil engineering.

Colour Plate 21 shows a surviving part of the wall around London. It is as solid as the day it was completed. So obviously is this not a quick-fix solution to a military emergency that the thinking now tends towards the idea that the wall was not built until the upstart emperor from Britain had been beaten in battle and died by his own hand. After seeing off any contestants for the throne, of whom the governor of Britain was but one, Severus was minded to impose his authority and show that he was not a man to be trifled with. He dispatched one of his cronies to govern Britain and it could well be that it was not until this time that London's wall was built.

Let us look closely at the wall around built around London at the end of the second or beginning of the third century AD and see if there are any clues about when and why it was built. We know that it was not erected any earlier than AD 190, because of the finding of a coin of this date. We also know that it could not have been built later than AD 210 or so.

This date is fixed by the discovery of some moulds for forging coins. Albinus, the governor of Britain, and Severus, who became emperor, were allies until at least AD 194. If Albinus was planning to launch a war and was minded to protect his capital city from attack beforehand by building a wall around it, then he was certainly cutting things a bit fine. As remarked, this wall would have taken at least two years to complete. Albinus crossed the Channel and proclaimed himself emperor in the autumn of AD 196, which means work would have to have started two years earlier, at the time that he and Severus were on good terms.

The real question to ask ourselves is whether or not what we can see of the Roman wall in London suggests some hastily built structure thrown up as a temporary expedient in time of war or preparation for war. Or does it, on the other hand, appear to be a beautifully constructed, well-planned piece of work about which there was no hurry at all and the only criterion was that it should be as well made as possible? Look again at Colour Plate 21. If the algae and moss were cleared away and the stonework scrubbed clean, this is a structure that could have been built last year. It is in perfect condition. It is hard to imagine that anything knocked together as a temporary response to some emergency almost 2000 years ago could possibly be in such good shape today. The blocks of stone are neatly shaped, the courses regular and the layers of brick to ensure stability are all precisely laid. For comparison, we turn to the medieval wall built on top of the Roman one. Here, ragged lumps of stone have been mortared together in a confused fashion which puts on in mind of crazy paving. This wall was built roughly a thousand years later than the Roman one and yet is in a pitiful condition, ready in places to topple down. If the Roman wall were anything like this, we might perhaps be justified in supposing that it was a hasty, stopgap measure. In fact, we have only to examine it carefully to realise that it was nothing of the sort. This wall was built calmly and carefully for a purpose. What was that purpose?

A number of walls were being built around British cities at this time and it would be rash to assume that all had the same motives behind them. In our own era we saw a wall which encircled the city of West Berlin. This was not, of course, built by those living in the city with the intention of keeping out intruders. Without fully understanding the context, it can sometimes be hard to work out the motive for a high wall. Which brings us back to the Roman walls in Britain and in particular the one around London.

There were probably two very different reasons for the wall around London; neither of which had any reference to defence or indeed any military consideration at all. Mention was made earlier in the chapter of Hadrian's Wall, which was essentially a border. The purpose of marking a border in the modern world is to make a statement to neighbouring territories: 'You may come this far and not an inch further'. The borders themselves are usually symbolic, although they can be reinforced with minefields, barbed wire and machine-gun posts. Even heavily fortified borders like this are not really meant to withstand an assault by a determined and heavily armed enemy. They signify more than here is somebody with whom it would be unwise to tangle.

Ordinary borders between nations are not supposed to withstand armies; they are intended to keep an eye upon who is going in and out of the country and to check that tax and customs duties are being correctly levied on goods passing through the border. These two motives, firstly to send a message to others that here is a country to be feared and respected and, secondly, the desire to collect taxes and keep an eye on people, were probably behind both Hadrian's Wall and the wall around London.

In a country where the tallest buildings of the indigenous inhabitants are little more than mud huts, the sight of a 20ft-high masonry wall with heavily armed soldiers marching up and down along it would be the ancient equivalent of the border between East and West Germany during the Cold War. It was a symbol of power. It tells anybody, from the casual traveller to an enemy insurgent: 'Do not mess with us, watch your step'. At the same time, this barrier makes sure that anything brought into or taken out of the country can be checked. If you are importing wine, there is a tax to be paid on it. You would be ill advised to try to smuggle weapons into the country; they will be found at the border. Precious metals are a government monopoly, so don't try to export them without declaring them at customs. Large sums of ready cash will invite questioning. All these principles are understood by today's border guards and things were pretty much the same at the border between Scotland and England or the barrier separating the port of London from the rest of the country.

After the emperor Severus had disposed of the imperial pretensions of the British governor, he dispatched as procurator to Britain a relative of his own by marriage. This man's task was twofold. First, he was to root out any other subversion in the province, find anybody else who might feel that it was worthwhile taking troops to Europe and challenging the authority of the emperor. His other task was to make sure that revenue from Britain began flowing once more towards Rome. Governors of Britain had been getting into the way of seeing themselves as independent rulers, rather than as running the country on behalf of an emperor thousands of miles away. Commodus had been exceedingly extravagant and when Severus assumed the office of emperor, he found that the imperial coffers were not as full as he might have hoped. This was something which had to be rectified as a matter of his own survival. He seized a good deal of property in Gaul from those whom he supposed to be his enemies and it is quite possible that he did the same thing in Britain.

We have seen that a recurring theme of the Roman Empire was that the individual with the backing of enough military units was generally the one who was able to secure the throne for himself. This meant that emperors became very cautious about allowing governors to have control of too many troops; it was this mindset which was partly responsible for the invasion of Britain in the first place. Roman soldiers were no different from most soldiers today. They tended to have little concern with abstract questions of political philosophy, being more interested in having money in their pockets, food in their bellies and good conditions in their barracks. In short, to keep your soldiers on your side, it was vital that you had plenty of money to pass onto them. Otherwise, you were apt to find that their loyalty wavered and if your rival could offer them more, then you might find yourself facing desertions and mutiny.

Having defeated his two most dangerous rivals, Niger and Albinus, Severus now needed to consolidate his position by passing his success on to his soldiers. To impress these men, this success would need to be in the practical form of money. In other words, Severus needed to start raising the imperial income by exploiting the provinces and making sure that all taxes and duties in the far off parts of the empire were collected and then forwarded promptly to Rome. This was most urgent, because as we saw above, Commodus had virtually bankrupted the imperial treasury by his extravagance. Another pressing task was to make sure that provincial governors like Niger and Albinus were not in the future able to rely upon the backing of 10 legions or so if they developed imperial ambitions and felt minded to march on Rome. This was a relatively simple task which entailed splitting up the provinces into smaller units; having two governors where before there was only one.

For Britain, there were two practical results of Severus' financial worries and anxieties about future revolts. He dispatched a new governor and as procurator he sent a young relative of his by marriage, Varius Marcellus. Now, of course, the first job facing the new administration would be to root out sedition and deal with any prominent supporters of the previous governor. Doubtless there were summary arrests and executions. It is also quite likely, at least judging by the actions already taken in mainland Europe, that quite a bit of private property was seized for the benefit of the imperial purse. There is evidence that some villas in Britain changed hands at this time. This was no more than opportunistic pilfering; it was not likely to increase revenues from Britain in the long run. Which is where London's wall comes into the picture.

London was where most imports arrived in the country and also where goods were shipped out to the continent. Then, as now, the government expected a cut of all these transactions in the form of taxes, customs and duties. How to ensure that these were not being evaded? Also, having collected the money, how to make quite sure that it gets to Rome and is not used to finance foreign adventures and attempts upon the throne? The second problem is easy enough to solve; you appoint some young relative of your wife's, a man who will be grateful for his elevation and seek to serve you loyally. The other difficulty can only be tackled by a long-term solution. If you physically enclose your docks and make sure that any cargoes entering or leaving the area are checked by government officials, then you are making a good start. Of course, you cannot stop smuggling entirely; that is never going to be a practical idea. What you can do, though, is make damned sure that if somebody arrives at London with a cartload of lead ingots from the West Country, intended for export to Europe, that they have to pass through a gateway where the load can be examined, recorded and the appropriate tax paid.

Having a wall round the city of London made it immeasurably easier for the staff of the procurator to keep track of who was coming in and out of the city and what they were bringing with them. While having the appearance of a benevolent measure to protect the citizens from some ill-defined enemy, the wall in fact made it possible to keep a watch on the people and record their comings and goings. This was obviously beneficial for the administration when collecting taxes and duties, but also in a more general way for keeping an eye out for plots and subversion. It is worth noting that the next procurator whom Severus appointed was the former head of his secret police; a man who was less renowned for his skill with figures than for his ability to sniff out subversion and uncover plots.

The wall was also a symbol of power and prestige. This was a city to take notice of; a mighty fortress, girded round with a wall which would not be out of place encircling a castle. The photograph in Colour Plate 22 shows the wall today at its greatest height. Even today, a couple of thousand years or so later, it is an impressive sight. The message of power and strength is amply conveyed. Both here and at Hadrian's Wall the message is loud and clear. People capable of throwing up walls like this are a force to be reckoned with. These walls are advertisements which proclaim loudly: we are strong, we are powerful, watch your step if you tangle with us.

Of course, history is never quite as simple as we hope and it is only fair to draw readers' attention at this point to a fragment of archaeological evidence which militates against the notion that London's wall was only designed to control the citizens and make sure that nobody dodged their taxes. The west and north walls of the fort became part of the external wall round the whole city. These walls were thickened from the inside in order to bring them up to the same strength as the rest of the city walls. Near to the Museum of London is a section of the foundation of the west wall of the fort. It can clearly be seen that this is really two walls; the thinner one is the original wall of the fort and the more sturdy part is the city wall which was built next to it. The photograph in Colour Plate 23 shows this. The apparent groove or channel on the left is where the two walls meet. On the left is the external west wall of the fort and on the right the thickening built at the same time as the rest of the city wall. Clearly, if the aim of the wall was not defensive and was simply to funnel traffic through one of the gates, there would have been no need for this thickening; the fort wall was quite adequate for the purpose. It such little mysteries as this that make up the very stuff of history.

The second consequence for Britain of Severus' suspicious nature and desire to prevent any future rebellions starting in this country was the division of the province of Britain into two parts: Britannia Superior in the south, with London as its capital, and Britannia Inferior in the north, with York as its major city. The intention was that nobody in Britain should again have three legions at his personal disposal. The same precaution was later taken in Syria. From this time on, London ceased to be the capital of Britain and was only the chief city of a smaller part of the province.

Third- and Fourth-century London

We shall, in this chapter, be covering a period of almost 200 years; approximately half the lifetime of the Roman city of London. There are few references to London by contemporary writers during this time and so we must extrapolate from written records concerning other parts of Britain and also rely heavily upon the archaeological evidence to see what life was like in the city from the beginning of the third until the end of the fourth century AD.

One theme which emerges during this time is a tendency for leaders in Britain to become ambitious and attempt to use the province as a power base, either to wrest control of the island from Rome or to use it as a springboard for their designs upon either the whole or part of the empire. It will be remembered from Chapter 1 that when Claudius invaded, he hoped to use Britain as a means of splitting up armies in Western Europe and preventing them from becoming so large that their commanders might be tempted to march on Rome and seize power. The idea was that having three legions based in this country would prevent those troops at least from becoming embroiled in intrigues which threatened the stability and good order of the empire. However, the legions in Britain were themselves a powerful military force. Being isolated geographically from the rest of the empire did seem to encourage imperial ambitions in the centuries after Clodius Albinus tried to take the throne.

The attitude of the army was, during these centuries, crucial. They could make or break both leaders in this country and also emperors in Rome. Shortly after he had defeated Albinus, Septimus Severus found the Roman army in Europe becoming a little restless and undisciplined. This was alarming and Severus found an ideal solution by gathering up as many troops as he could muster and taking them to Britain. Far better that they should cool their blood fighting the savages in Scotland than that they should have the leisure to sit around in the barracks seeing if they could think of anybody who would make a better emperor than the one that they actually had. This parlour game would have been particularly hazardous for Severus, since he had two ambitious and unruly sons, one of whom was counting the time until he could himself take over the empire. Young men of this sort sometimes provide a natural focus for discontented elements in the armed forces.

All other considerations aside, there were sound political and pragmatic reasons for visiting Britain in this way. It would in the first place do the British no harm to see the triumphant emperor that had defeated their leader arrive in town with a huge army behind him. It might remind them of the folly of trying to declare war on the legitimate emperor again in a hurry. Secondly, the tribes beyond Hadrian's Wall were becoming a little too daring in their defiance of Rome and it would do them no harm either to be reminded who was boss. Severus also needed to appear as a strong military leader. The fact that he was not very robust and needed to be carried in a litter rather than being able to ride on horseback made this especially important for him. It never did for any of the emperors to appear weak or unable to hold their own during military campaigning. This was an open invitation for some enterprising subordinate to assassinate him and seize control himself. We need only look at the events following Severus' death to see the dangers for weak-looking emperors. Caracalla, who became emperor, was himself murdered by one of his bodyguards. In the next 40 years, no fewer than 55 emperors were proclaimed; many lasted only days before they were murdered by ambitious rivals.

Severus' first port of call was London. He made two very shrewd decisions while staying in the city. The first of these was to leave his son Geta in control of the empire when he headed north to deal with the unrest in Scotland. The young man had never been given any responsibility before, but Severus left him, advised by a council of ministers, more or less in charge of the empire. The more dangerous and power hungry of his two sons, Caracalla, he took with him on the military campaign so that he could keep an eye on him. The fighting in Scotland was indecisive, with Severus and his army unable to lure the British tribesmen into the kind of pitched battle that the Roman army excelled at. The most that he was able to do was force the Britons to acknowledge his authority and promise to behave themselves in the future. Needless to say, as soon as he left Scotland, it was business as usual for the warriors in the north and their agreements were swiftly forgotten.

In AD 209, Severus ordered the army back into Scotland. This time they were on a purely punitive expedition, killing more or less at random. Severus himself was not a well man and stayed in York during this time. It is possible that he handed over control of the army to his son Caracalla.

Meanwhile, Geta was ruling the empire in his father's absence, holding a post roughly analogous to that of regent. He was, in effect, the acting emperor; a fact which his ruthless brother was unable either to forgive or forget when once their father died.

In February 210, Severus died at York. Geta and Caracalla became joint emperors, which lasted until they got back to Rome, where Caracalla had his brother murdered. In AD 212 or 214 Caracalla made a proclamation as emperor which had a profound effect upon London. This was the *Constitution Antoniniana*, more commonly known as the Edict of Caracalla. This granted full Roman citizenship to all free men in the empire. Although an apparently wide-ranging and open-ended offer, in practice this applied only to cities. Only in the cities of the Roman Empire was Roman law fully enforced. This, of course, tied in with the whole notion of civilisation as being synonymous with city life. Provincial cities such as London were the main beneficiaries of the Edict of Caracalla. Full Roman citizenship had been more a feature of those living in Italian cities before this edict; now everybody living in London who was not a slave could be considered a citizen.

The consequences of one of Severus' actions lingered on after his death like a ticking time bomb which ultimately led to dreadful consequences for both Britain itself and the empire as a whole. Having discovered when he became emperor that Commodus' excesses had bankrupted the imperial treasury, Severus hit upon what seemed to him an very cunning plan to keep the books balanced. Obviously, one of the first things he had to do as emperor was to make the army happy by increasing their pay. How to do this with little hard currency at his disposal? His solution was a simple if short-sighted one. He devalued the currency, reducing by two-thirds the amount of silver in the coins which he used to pay the troops. This produced, as might reasonably have been expected, inflation, which eventually caused great harm to the empire's economy.

Britain itself was heading for something of a Golden Age, although it wouldn't have looked like that at the time. In AD 259, after a succession of dozens of different emperors whose reigns lasted only days, weeks or at best months before they were murdered or deposed, a leader called Postumus established the league of Gallic provinces, including Britain, into a separate little empire called the *Imperium Galliarum*. This enterprise lasted for just 15 years until the emperor Aurelian brought Britain back into the fold of the main Roman Empire. Just two years later, in AD 276, Gaul was attacked by barbarians from the north who overran more than 50 towns. In the French countryside many villas were abandoned at this time and never reoccupied. Although there were incursions by Saxon pirates, the presence of the North Sea insulated Britain from the worst of these disturbances. The villas of Gaul may have been falling into ruin, but those in this country were flourishing as never before. Britain and London had never been so well off.

London underwent something of a resurgence at this time. The part of the city to the west of the Walbrook had been given over to agriculture and many of the workshops and houses there had been demolished. A programme of rebuilding was now embarked upon, of which this district was the focus. Marshy land was drained and the ground stabilised for new buildings. Many of these buildings were elaborate, with beautiful mosaics. It looks as though there was suddenly a lot more money floating around London. At the same time, a large area in the south-west of the walled city, south of St Paul's Cathedral, was the site of even greater building work. A temple complex was built there as well as a triumphal arch.

This sudden burst of activity and apparent prosperity affected not only London, but was evident also in the rest of Britain. Many villas in the British countryside were upgraded at this time, with new wings added and mosaic floors being laid. This laid the foundation for the so-called 'Golden Age' of the Roman villas in London, which took place in the first half of the fourth century.

A plausible explanation has been advanced which explains the new prosperity in Britain in economic terms as a consequence of what had been happening in Gaul. It is supposed that there was a 'flight of capital' from Gaul to Britain and that as the barbarians advanced, so well-off citizens in Gaul fled to this country, after having converted all their wealth into portable property, probably in the form of silver and gold. This is as good an explanation as any for all the building work which we see in both London and the countryside.

London may have been enjoying something of a boom, but the city could not wholly escape the storm clouds which were gathering elsewhere in Europe. True, the cities of Britain were not falling into the hands of barbarians as those of Gaul had done, but the country was still attracting unfavourable attention from seaborne raiders from the same area; namely northern Europe beyond the Rhine. These Saxons were not invaders, they were really more like pirates or brigands seeking what they could seize and carry off. They had no intention at this time of actually coming to live in this country. They must have sailed up the Thames at some point, because in the late third century, work began on a riverside wall which would protect the city from enemies arriving from the water.

We come now to a most peculiar episode in the history of Roman Britain, one which saw both the first mint being set up in London and also witnessed the city coming very close to being sacked by German mercenaries. This is the period during which the province of Britain was ruled by an adventurer from Gaul, who although technically an admiral in the Roman navy was himself little better than a pirate.

Before we look at the story of Carausius, we must first see how the Romans had fallen into the habit of employing some pretty dubious types in their armed forces. This trend, which was adopted by the British in later years, tended to lead to trouble. It had always been possible for non-Romans to join the Roman army. If the armed forces of the Republic and later the empire had been limited to those born in a certain part of Italy, then it would never have grown large enough to be able to maintain order throughout the known world of that time. So far, so good. A Roman unit containing Britons and Gauls, Greeks and Romans is fine. The difficulty comes when one begins to rely too heavily upon whole parts of the army which are made up of so-called barbarians. Such soldiers often had their own agenda, and their ambitions and loyalties did not necessarily coincide with those of the emperors who employed them. In the final years of the empire, this had catastrophic consequences, when whole armies of barbarians were fighting for Rome on a purely cash basis. These men were in effect mercenaries who could and did change sides if the situation required it.

In the fourth century, around a quarter of the Roman army were Germans and they rose to high rank, even becoming generals. Some Germans and those of other nationalities from outside the empire went back to their own countries after retirement with a comprehensive knowledge of the dispositions, tactics, strengths and weaknesses of the Roman army. They then passed this information on to others, who used it for their own ends.

Even before matters reached the stage of engaging whole bands of freebooters of doubtful loyalty, the empire had come to rely upon many men whose eye was more upon the main chance than it was the welfare and defence of the Roman Empire. Take M. Aurelius Mausaeus Carausius, a man of humble birth from that part of Gaul which is today Belgium. A soldier renowned for fighting against Gaulish brigands, he was given command of a fleet based in the Channel. Saxon pirates were sailing south at this time and raiding the coastal towns of Gaul. Carausius' brief was to protect the coast from these depredations and warn off the barbarians. At first, he seemed to enjoy great success, but after a while his activities began to look a little fishy. He always seemed to appear on the scene after the Saxons had carried out their attacks and set to sea again. His ships made contact with the marauders, but none of the loot was ever returned to the owners, nor was any treasure forwarded to Rome. The explanation was fairly simple. Carausius had cut a deal with the pirates, whereby he would take a percentage of what they stole, in return for which he allowed them to operate with impunity in the North Sea and English Channel. It was a nice little earner, but when Maximian the emperor in Rome, heard of it he ordered Carausius' immediate execution.

Some men would at this point have made a run for it and perhaps thrown in their lot with the pirates. Carausius was not such a one. His riposte to the sentence of death passed upon him was a bold and unexpected stroke of daring which left the whole empire gaping in reluctant admiration. In AD 286, he took the entire fleet over to Britain, where he proclaimed himself Emperor of Britain and Gaul. He was in fact reviving the idea of the *Imperium Galliarum* or Gallic Empire.

It is something of a mystery just why the British should have allowed this Gaul to land in their country and declare himself its ruler. True, he had a fleet of ships, but three legions were stationed in Britain. Presumably, he enjoyed the support of these legions, otherwise he would never have been able to assert his authority over the whole country. In AD 288, Emperor Maximian sent an invasion fleet to retake Britain, but Carausius defeated it at sea. For the next five years, he ruled in London as Emperor of the British and Gallic peoples. With the British legions backing him, Carausius seemed to be in an invincible position. He started a mint in London, the first ever to operate in the city.

Carausius used the coinage which he issued from London as a brilliant form of propaganda. Coins carried slogans such as *Restitutor Britanniae*, 'Restorer of Britain', and *Genius Britanniae*, 'Spirit of Britain'. All this was effective enough self-advertisement, but Carausius did not stop there. He reformed the currency entirely, reinstituting coins made of solid silver which had long ago vanished form the empire due to the debasement of the currency carried out shamelessly by a succession of emperors.

Carausius enjoyed pretending to be an emperor equal in status to the real one in Rome. For seven years, his court flourished in London and the inscriptions on his coins became more and more extravagant, describing Carausius as the 'Chosen One'. The man who advised him about financial matters and who might perhaps have originally hit upon the idea of producing new, pure silver coins, was his minister Allectus. In AD 293, Allectus murdered his master and managed to gain the allegiance of the army and rule for a further three years. By this time Constantius, the emperor in Rome, was ready and launched an invasion of Britain to bring it back into the Roman fold. This precipitated the most dangerous threat to London since Boudica had attacked the city over 300 years earlier.

Constantius' forces landed in southern Britain and swiftly disposed of Allectus and his regular forces who had marched south to meet them in battle. In addition to his army, Allectus had engaged many Frankish mercenaries and these fled from the field of battle in Hampshire and made for London. Their only aim now was to see what they could seize before returning to their own country. Allectus had taken all his troops with him when he left London to fight Constantius and the city lay defenceless before the barbarian hordes which descended upon it. They began to sack the city, killing and looting with no opposition at all. It was beginning to look like a repeat of Boudica's actions, when the city was unexpectedly saved. Constantius had held part of his invasion fleet in reserve and sent it round the coast to sail up the Thames, entering London and landing troops there to secure the capital. They arrived while the mercenaries were just getting into the swing of things and in the words of Eumenius, writing in the next century: 'the ships reached London, found survivors of the barbarian mercenaries plundering the city, and when these began to seek flight, landed and slew them in the streets.' Britain had been restored to the empire and a famous medallion was struck to commemorate this event. It shows Constantius on horseback and a female figure, the personification of London, kneeling before him in gratitude. This all sounds very touching, but it is possible that the emperor was less impressed with the thanks of the Londoners than this medal suggests.

Shortly after Britain was brought again under the control of Rome, London's magnificent basilica and forum were razed to the ground. Since these were among the largest buildings in Europe, there must have been a powerful reason for demolishing them at this time. It has been suggested that this action was taken to punish the British for their support of Carausius and his henchmen for so long. Another step taken at this time was the sub-division of Britain into four provinces. This was doubtless to try to prevent one commander in the country having too many forces at his disposal and seceding once more from the empire. London was to be the capital of only one part of Britain: *Maxima Caesariensis*.

The first half of the fourth century was a golden age for Britain. The country was prosperous and at peace. The villas in the countryside show this clearly and life in London was better than it had ever been. We know in ret-rospect that the Roman Empire's days were numbered and that Britain was about to enter the dark ages, but for Londoners in about AD 320, everything looked rosy.

There were warning signs for those who heeded them. In the empire as whole, the inflation caused by the regular debasement of the currency was eating away at the economy. Without any understanding of the very concept of inflation, though, nobody was tackling it. Britain had a more specific difficulty. The level of the River Thames had been dropping year after year, for reasons which need not concern us. The result of this was that the port itself was beginning to silt up and the tidal part of the river no longer reached as far upstream as London. This made it far harder to bring ships into the port. They couldn't simply ride in on the tide as had been done for centuries. The riverside wall might be handy to keep off pirates, but it made it harder to offload goods from the quays and move them straight into the warehouses. It might be good for defence, but it was ruinous for commerce. The economy of Britain began to suffer from the ill effects of their main port slowing down in this way. It would take decades for these effects to become serious, but in the meantime, life seemed to be going very smoothly for most.

This pleasant interlude was to come to an abrupt end in AD 367, when London once again came close to falling to an army of barbarians. This was a result of the so-called 'Barbarian Conspiracy'. Up until this time, most attacks by Scots, Irish, Germans and other nations on the fringes of the empire were of a random and haphazard nature. Sometimes, the activities of Saxon pirates became a little too much and on other occasions raids into Britain from the tribes north of Hadrian's Wall became a serious nuisance. All these events were, until AD 367, unco-ordinated. One might have to tackle Irish raiders one year and then deal with the Saxons the next. This was just about manageable.

We looked earlier in this chapter at the enlistment of foreigners in the Roman army and the increasing dependence of Rome upon German volunteers. As remarked, these soldiers often left the army and returned to their own countries with plenty of sensitive information about the military disposition of Roman forces. It cannot be doubted that leaks of this sort encouraged and may even have caused the attacks on Western Europe which took place in AD 367. Simultaneous seaborne raids began on the coast of Gaul by Saxons and Franks, while Britain itself was overrun from all directions. Tribesmen from Scotland crossed Hadrian's Wall in large numbers, Irish warriors landed in Britain and other bands of armed men, Saxons and Franks, arrived in East Anglia.

A number of walled towns in this country fell to the barbarian invaders, and Saxons entered London. The situation was exacerbated by desertions from the official Roman army. Many other soldiers, rather than deserting, insisted that they were just going on leave for a while. There seemed to be no appetite at all to face the invaders in battle and the army simply melted away, leaving both the towns and countryside defenceless. The Roman Empire was not prepared to sacrifice the province and so launched a counter-invasion of their own. By the time that the Romans landed in Kent, the Barbarian Conspiracy had degenerated into bands of brigands roaming across the British countryside, looting, raping, killing and pillaging as they went.

As the Roman forces moved towards London, they encountered many groups of men who were behaving like bandits. They were herding stolen cattle and had lines of chained prisoners, whom they obviously intended to export as slaves. The Romans dealt mercilessly with these characters, executing them on the spot. Where possible, they restored any goods recovered to the owners, a gesture which created much good will towards the army among the citizens of Britain. They were received in London with rapturous applause and genuine gratitude. For those living there, it must have seemed as though the end of the world had come and that they had been rescued just in the nick of time.

The commander of the Roman forces which rescued London issued a number of proclamations. A general pardon was announced for all deserters and those who had gone 'on leave' were recalled to the colours. This was an act of signal generosity, considering how harshly the Roman army usually dealt with deserters and mutineers. Long-term plans were also put into place for the future protection of London from attacks of this sort. Among these was the strengthening of the defences on the east side of the city. This took the form of the building of 20 bastions or semi-circular towers. These towers were in effect artillery positions, containing the most powerful weapon known to the Romans at that time, the catapult.

The catapult was like a giant crossbow, 10ft long. It fired an iron-tipped arrow with considerable force for a great distance. This was powerful enough to penetrate any armour. One of these machines was fitted in every one of the new towers built on to London's walls. The installation and use of these weapons has been associated with the presence of German mercenaries, but this is a debateable point. We do know that the towers were built, because the traces of them still remains, most notably at a section of the wall about half a mile north of the Tower of London.

Work also carried out on the riverside wall was also completed at about this time, so that London was now entirely surrounded with fortifications. The quality of the later sections of this wall, built at this time, is very poor. It shows every sign of being erected in a hurry with no proper foundations at all. Lumps of stone of all sorts are rammed into the clay of the riverbank and fixed together with mortar. Old pagan altars, tombstones, pieces of a monumental arch; all are just piled up in a jumble to provide some sort of barrier against those attempting to enter the city from the Thames.

While all this was going on in London, coastal defences were also being strengthened. It is plain that the threat to London was believed to be coming from the east coast. There has been a lot of debate about the apparent evidence for large numbers of German soldiers, perhaps employed by the British as mercenaries at this time. Most of this centres around burials in the Thames valley of men who were interred with distinctive belt buckles which indicated a German origin. If it is true that the British were engaging large numbers of such mercenaries at that time, then the implications may be far reaching. These men would have come from roughly the same area as the Saxon pirates who were menacing the east of Britain. Did the pirates and raiders have friends and relatives serving with the army in Britain? Is that what made this an attractive country to settle in; that they already had connections living here? Could it be the employing German mercenaries to protect London actually acted in the long run as a magnet which drew other Germans to come to this country and stay?

In AD 383 the leader of Britain was a Spanish man called Magnus Maximus. He enjoyed the support of the army and, like other British leaders before in this position, decided to make an attempt for independence. At the same time, he evidently had it in mind to restart the Gallic Empire. He moved troops to Gaul and for a while seemed to be in control of a section of Western Europe. His rule lasted only three years.

The Last Londoners

We have watched Londinium rise and fall, being devastated by fire not once but twice in the first hundred years of its existence. The city's population has grown and fallen and it has expanded and shrunk accordingly. By the end of the fourth century, London was far less important than it had once been and its commercial life considerably less vigorous. In a sense, those living in the city at this time would have felt under siege and more than a little beleaguered by forces beyond their control. The riverside wall had been completed, which interfered with the running of the port, and they had come close to having their city sacked by the disaffected forces of Allectus. Britain had seen off the invasion of the Franks, Irish and Attacotti, the so-called Barbarian Conspiracy of AD 367, but over them still hung the threat of attack by Saxon pirates and other brigands from Germany and those northern parts of Europe which had never been part of the Roman Empire.

It is not to be supposed, though, that this was anything like a dark age for Roman London. Quite the contrary. Trade was still taking place with the continent and the luxury goods upon which expatriate Romans and Romanised Celts had come to depend for their lifestyle were still getting through. We saw that the first homes in London were little better than mud huts and we then observed that London was rebuilt after the Boudican disaster as a planned, Roman city. The standard of living rose and governors like Agricola encouraged the Britons to share in the Roman way of life and adopt the customs of civilisation. The mud floors had given way to simple red tesserae, which in turn laid the way for mosaics and painted walls. The way of life in London as the fifth century dawned was infinitely better than that of only a few centuries earlier. The city might have shrunk and be past its prime, but life there was a good deal more comfortable than a host of other places in ancient Europe. Yet in the east, storm clouds were gathering which would ultimately sweep all this away and reduce the whole country to a way of life more primitive than that which Claudius found when he invaded Britain in AD 43.

The collapse of Roman London did not happen overnight. It was not an event, so much as a process. Like the end of the Roman Empire itself, it happened over the course of many years and those living in the city would have been hard pressed to identify a particular moment when Londinium came to an end. It was not sacked by invaders, nor destroyed in a catastrophe. It simply faded quietly away.

We may not be able to date precisely the end of the Roman Empire or of its province Britannia, but we know pretty well when the process of dissolution began which ended in Britain being sundered from Rome for good. In Chapter 1 we read what Thucydides said: 'empires cannot remain stagnant; they must grow'. As the fifth century began, centuries had passed since Rome's empire had grown any larger. The name of the game had been for many years consolidation; hanging on to what they already had rather than seeking new territories to conquer. One of the natural borders to the Roman Empire was historically the Rhine. This river separated the civilised Roman provinces from the German barbarians to the north.

The winter of 406/407 was bitterly cold. Perhaps due to hunger in the north of Europe caused by the harsh weather or perhaps for another reason, large groups of tribesmen began gathering on the bank of the Rhine as the end of AD 406 drew near. On the last day of the year, the river froze over completely and within hours the barbarian hordes were sweeping south into Gaul. There were two practical consequences of this invasion. The first was that communications between London and Rome were disrupted. The fear in Britain was that the barbarians would soon turn their attention to this country. After all, anybody standing on the seashore near Boulogne can see the cliffs of Dover. The leadership in London did not need much imagination to see that once the various tribes had carved out little kingdoms for themselves in Gaul, they could easily turn their attention to Britain.

Although nominally still under the hegemony of Rome, the army in Britain had been appointing and deposing the country's leaders at will. Early in AD 406 they had set up a soldier called Marcus and then murdered him a few months later when he seemed to them not to be up to the job. The army then installed an urban councillor called Gratian as leader, only to find him unsatisfactory in the post. He lasted a mere four months before also being assassinated by discontented soldiers. It is surprising, given the high mortality rate for the post, that the army were able to find any takers after Gratian, but the next man who took the job, a soldier called Constantine, seemed to be able to handle things a little better. He was an ambitious man and promised the army both money and prestige, which was just what they wanted.

Following in the footsteps of Clodius Albinus in AD 196 and Magnus Maximus in AD 383, Constantine quickly decided to make an attempt on the throne and took the army across the Channel to Gaul. He carved out for himself a miniature empire consisting of Gaul and Spain. His actions certainly discouraged the barbarians from heading towards Britain; they turned south instead. To that extent, Constantine's adventure was to the benefit of this country. It at least delayed the inevitable for a few months. While their leader was away in Europe with the army, though, playing at being a prince, Britain was left unguarded to other enemies and in AD 408 a Saxon invasion of southern Britain took place. It was eventually repelled, but those leaders left in Britain decided that they were better off tackling their own difficulties without the aid of either their nominal leader Constantine or the distant imperial capital in Rome. They declared themselves to be independent of the Roman Empire. The following year, the emperor Honorius wrote to the cities of Britain, there no longer being any central authority, and told them that they would have to make arrangements for their own defence. They could expect no further help from Rome. The Romans had their own problems. In the same year that Honorius warned the British to look to their own defence, Rome itself was sacked by the Goths under the leadership of Alaric.

What was happening in London during these tumultuous events? The evidence suggests that life in the British cities continued much as before. Society was run in the Roman way and those living in the cities like London thought of themselves in a sense as Romans rather than Britons. Buildings were still being repaired, drains laid, town councils still met. Individual groups of invaders were certainly landing in Britain during this time, but they tended to bypass the walled cities. This was not an army seeking to engage in siege warfare, but something more akin to groups of bandits seeing what they could pick up for nothing. Some of them began settling and starting farms of their own, but even so, life carried on in places like London more or less as usual.

It was at one time thought that the end of cities like London was a matter of barbarian hordes reducing the defences by force of arms and then looting and pillaging. There is no evidence at all that this happened. To be sure, there were fires during this time which destroyed parts of some cities. Fortifications were damaged too and defensive walls pulled down. Such destruction was in general wrought upon cities that were already deserted. Travellers sheltering in an empty house might inadvertently allow a cooking fire to get out of control, with disastrous consequences. A farmer might pull stones from an abandoned wall and use them to build a hut. The fabric of early churches often incorporated Roman remains; we can see this in London with the Saxon arch at All Hallows by the Tower church. The Saxons, Angles and Jutes who were arriving did not like cities and gave them a wide berth. Thirty years after Britain had declared its independence from Rome, a water main in the traditional Roman style was being laid in St Albans. There at least it was business as usual in the town. In London, a second-century house which had been extensively rebuilt in the fourth century was still occupied in around AD 440. Part of an amphora from the eastern Mediterranean was found there; so supplies of luxury goods were still reaching London in the middle of the fifth century. There is reason to suppose that a bathhouse attached to the house was also in use at this time.

The picture is one of gradual decay and abandonment rather than conquest by the edge of the sword. The citizens of London may have felt under pressure but this is more likely to have been because supplies of olive oil and wine were not getting across the Channel rather than because armed men were besieging their city walls. St Germanus visited Britain several times in the first half of the fifth century and apparently found the cities functioning perfectly normally. There is other evidence that at late as AD 450, almost half a century after Britain ceased to be a Roman province, the leaders in the country, particularly those from the cities, still felt a powerful sense of identification with Rome. According to the Welsh monk Gildas, for instance, writing in the sixth century, Britain appealed one last time to Rome for military help. After spending centuries under the yoke of Rome, the British were inviting the Roman army back into their country, feeling that they had more in common with Rome than they did the north Europeans who were now arriving in ever-increasing numbers. Gildas records the message sent to Rome as follows: 'the barbarians push us into the sea, the sea pushes us back to the barbarians; between these two sorts of death, we are either slaughtered or drowned.'

Gildas tells us that this appeal for help, known as 'The Groans of the Britons', was dispatched to Rome in AD 449. Six years later, Britain was still in close contact with Rome, at least in religious matters. In AD 455, the Roman Church agreed to change the date of Easter. The Church in Britain adopted this change, showing clearly that they were still in contact with, and part of, the wider communion. However, changes made in Roman liturgy and practice after this date were not observed in Britain. This, combined with Gildas' records, fixes pretty precisely the time when contact was finally lost between Rome and the cities of Britain. We know from the archaeological record that by the end of the fifth century, London was all but deserted and fast becoming ruinous. The first trace of Saxon activity in the city is a brooch which was dropped by some wanderer in the bathhouse of a house in Billingsgate. The style suggests that this brooch was made no later than about AD 430.

There is one final and tantalising piece of archaeological evidence which might point to the survival of Roman civilisation in London for longer than has previously been suspected. In 2006, the vaults beneath the church of St Martin in the Fields were excavated. A number of intriguing discoveries were made; not least of a stone sarcophagus from the fourth century which might indicate an early Christian burial in the London area. More to the point here was that a Roman tile kiln was found, which had seemingly been built between AD 400 and 450. The implication is that some Romans or Romanised Celts were still at work in London during this period, repairing houses and perhaps putting up new buildings. One would hardly bother to set up a kiln of this sort if the place was falling to pieces and the city was on the point of being abandoned. Whoever was at work here obviously thought that there was some practical point in turning out Roman-style tiles on an industrial scale. This kiln is the last structure in London which we can be sure was erected during the Roman period.

The end of Roman life in London did not, as we have seen, come about in a tempest of fire and swordplay. It was once thought that the cities and towns of Roman Britain fell to the invaders, who sacked them as Boudica had once sacked Colchester, London and St Albans. It is possible that this was the fate which befell some isolated villas, but the Saxons had neither the patience nor the technical expertise to reduce walled cities by siege warfare. Why should they bother? There was nothing for them in the cities; they were more interested in rich farmland or undefended homes.

It must have been a sad decline for those who chose to carry on living in London during the fifth century. Some residents would perhaps have moved west to try and make contact with communities of Romanised Celts who were resisting the Saxons. Others might have taken ship for Europe. Each departure of this sort would mean the permanent and irreversible dwindling of the city's population. Those that remained would have the city to themselves. Towards the end, entire blocks and streets would have been deserted. There was no pressure from the invading Saxons; simply that those supplies necessary for the maintenance of a Roman, city lifestyle, were no longer arriving in London.

13

The Deserted City

By AD 500 almost the whole of eastern England, including London, was under Anglo-Saxon control. One might have thought that a defensible area containing a number of stone buildings and a huge quantity of building material such as bricks, tiles and stone blocks would have been a perfect place for Saxons to settle and establish their own town. For some reason, though, they avoided the Roman city of London entirely for centuries. Perhaps they were gripped by some superstitious dread; the fear of those who had once ruled the whole world and been capable of casually building great walls which were twice the height of any Saxon house. An Anglo-Saxon poet, writing in England at this time, said:

> Wondrous is this wall-stone,
> Broken by fate, the castles have decayed,
> The work of giants is crumbling.

'The work of giants.' There are other references to this legend in Anglo-Saxon writings; that the mighty walls and buildings which they encountered had not been made by human hands, but by a race of giants who once lived in this island. It must be borne in mind that the Angles and Saxons came from outside the Roman Empire and were not at all familiar with cities. For most of these simple peasants from beyond the Rhine, their first sight of tall stone buildings must have been awe inspiring.

That some taboo must have been at work concerning living and work-ing in the ruins of the ancient city may be seen from the way in which the Saxons ignored the existing port of London, the wharfs and quays which lined the river bank between Tower Hill and the Walbrook. They chose instead to start completely from scratch, making a new port of their own a few miles upstream from the city of London. Near to this port they started their own settlement. This area, stretching roughly from the mouth of the Fleet to Westminster, was called Lundenwic. In recent years, there have been many finds from this period between the Strand and the Thames and also in Aldwych, which means in Anglo-Saxon, 'old port'. In contrast to this, hardly any evidence of Saxon occupation has emerged from the city of London from the years between about AD 450 and 750. All the archaeological data suggests that the place was practically deserted during those three centuries. Evidence of many buildings from the period between the seventh and ninth centuries has been discovered in the area west of the River Fleet, as far as Westminster. In an area of roughly comparable size to the east of the Fleet, the old walled city, hardly any such buildings have been found.

There is one notable exception to the trend mentioned above. The only remaining Saxon structure in the whole of London is to be found not in the Strand or Aldwych, but in the easternmost part of the City of London; that area delineated by the Roman wall. It is in the church of All Hallows by the Tower, near to the Tower of London, that a fine Saxon arch survives. One glance at it and it can at once be seen that this archway was built of material scavenged from the decaying Roman buildings which must then have surrounded the site: red tiles and old bits of ragstone, all held together by rough mortar. This arch is part of a church that was founded here around AD 750. There seems no particular reason to have built a church here, miles from the main settlement of Saxon London, but here it is.

Roman London was by and large a place through which one passed to gain access to the new areas of settlement. A Saxon road passed through the walled city from Essex, via Lundenwic, to the West Country. This road entered Roman London at Aldgate and left the city at Ludgate. Instead of passing between those two gates in a straight line, the road curves south for some distance after Aldgate. We can follow the line of the Saxon road by looking at modern-day Fenchurch Street and Lombard Street. The most likely explanation for this detour is that it avoided the ruins of the forum which once stood where Leadenhall Market is now. All of which suggests that the ruins of Roman London were treated with some degree of awe. One threaded a path between them, rather than lingering in the area long enough to loot or destroy them. One also hesitated simply to drive a road across the remains of the old buildings, treating them instead with respect and weaving between them.

This feeling of reverence for the remnants of a city, the like of which none of these people could really imagine any ordinary humans building or living in, lasted for centuries. The taboo that the walled city itself was somehow sacred, haunted or unwholesome gradually wore off after 200 or 300 years. Eventually, later generations would use the stones and tiles of the ancient temples and bathhouses to build Christian churches.

In AD 886 King Alfred re-established settlement in the old walled city. This followed the abandonment of Lundenwic 30 years earlier, caused by constant Viking raids up the Thames. It is plain that Roman buildings were still standing at that time, as can be seen from contemporary writings. Three years after Alfred ordered the reoccupation of London, a document refers to 'an old stone building known as Hwaetmundestan'. Judging from the location, this probably refers to one of the Roman bathhouses.

This then was the final end of Roman London. After centuries of neglect, the area within the walls was tidied up, the old buildings demolished and a new city begun. Londinium had ceased to exist and had been replaced by London.

14

Exploring Roman London

A surprising amount of Roman London is still visible, if one only knows where to look. The remains are scattered and fragmentary and yet enough exist to give a feel for the ancient city which lies beneath modern London. Perhaps the best place to begin is one of the earliest surviving structures: the fort built at the beginning of the second century AD.

About halfway along Noble Street in the City of London, a stone's throw from London's wall, is an old bomb site left over from the Second World War. This small strip of ruined old buildings overgrown with weeds contains enough of the Roman fort to give us an idea of its shape and general plan. We start by standing at the end of this sunken garden, just where Oat Lane joins Noble Street. Looking down, we see a square stone foundation, with a curved wall leading from it. This is the corner turret of the Roman fort, which was built around AD 125.

This fort was built in what is known as the 'playing card' design; so-called because the corners are curved rather than sharply angled. Colour Plate 18 shows this and also indicated the corner of the fort at which we are now looking, which is shown in the photograph in Colour Plate 19. The west wall of the fort followed the line of the old Victorian brick walls which run towards London Wall. Before we follow the line of the fort's wall, look closely at the foundation of the turret. Extending away on the opposite side from where we stand is a mass of Roman masonry. This is the city wall which was built in about AD 200. It incorporated the west and north wall of the fort in its circuit. Those walls of the fort were strengthened internally, to bring them up to the same thickness as the rest of the city wall. If we walk along Noble Street, we can see the Roman stonework upon which these walls were built. The foundation of another of the internal turrets may be seen. Crossing London Wall and entering the gardens next to the Museum of London, we will find a semi-circular bastion or tower. This dates from the reign of Henry III, a thousand years after the fort was completed. Along the straight edge of the semi-circular foundation are the remains of the Roman wall of the fort. One can see the characteristic red tiles embedded within the Kentish ragstone blocks. Looking to the left-hand end of this short section of wall reveals something curious.

A narrow channel or groove runs along the length of Roman wall. This is actually the division between two separate walls, built 80 years apart. The wall on the far side of the groove was the original wall of the fort. This may clearly be seen in the photograph in Colour Plate 23. At the end of the second century, between AD 190 and 220, a wall was erected which enclosed the entire city. The west and north walls of the fort became part of the outer wall of the city and were strengthened and thickened. What we see here is the gap between the original wall and the new and stronger city wall which was built against the wall of the fort.

To our left is the west gate of the Roman fort and once a month the Museum of London arranges guided tours of what is left of the gateway, which now lies buried beneath a car park. The guardroom and other features are visible and it is well worth making the effort to join one of these tours. The line of the fort wall stretches on, towards an ornamental lake in the Barbican development. If we continue walking in that direction, that is to say away from Noble Street, we come to another semi-circular tower on the edge of the water. This enables us to gauge the exact size of the Roman fort. This was the north-west corner of the fort and if we look back in the direction of Noble Street, then the distance from the internal turret at which we first looked gives us the length of the sides of this square fort. For unknown reasons, the fort stopped being used for military purposes at around the same time that the city wall was constructed.

Near the fort was an amphitheatre, which was discovered in 1988. It had been hypothesised for years that London must have had its own amphitheatre and during building work in 1951, a small section of a curved Roman wall was seen near to the Guildhall. The discovery in 1988 of more curved walls confirmed that this was indeed the location of the long-lost amphitheatre. When the new Guildhall art gallery was being built from 1992 onwards, the opportunity was taken to excavate fully the walls which had been uncovered a few years previously and the east end of the arena was revealed, including the entrance used by gladiators and others entering the ring. It is now possible for visitors to walk along this same path into the arena. A wooden drain was found running along this route and this has been carefully preserved in situ.

Excavating and preserving these remains was an astonishing feat of engineering. Although they lay in the basement of the art gallery, at the Roman ground level, another basement has been dug beneath them.

An earth and timber arena stood here for some decades, before being replaced by the present structure in the early second century, built at roughly the same time as the nearby fort. This amphitheatre could seat 6000 spectators – perhaps as many as a third of the city's population. A curious feature of the amphitheatre is the profound effect it had upon the layout of medieval London in this district. Even today, the actual area of the arena is still an open space and has never been built upon. It is perhaps not a coincidence that the Guildhall began on the edge of this open space. It has been suggested that in Saxon times, the disused amphitheatre was used as a convenient meeting place and that because of this, the official meeting hall was established nearby.

Walking into the arena along the original entranceway is a strange experience. The sand and gravel which lies alongside the walls is the original surface which was still in place when the remains were found.

It is still possible to visit a fairly typical second-century home which was built in the easternmost part of Londinium. It is to be found in the basement of All Hallows by the Tower church. This is, incidentally, the oldest church in London. Bomb damage during the Second World War destroyed part of a wall, uncovering a Saxon archway from the seventh century. This is the only Saxon structure in the entire city. In the crypt of this church it is possible to walk across a perfectly preserved red tesserae pavement which once formed the floor of the Roman house which stood here before the Saxons built a church upon the site.

Entering the crypt, one can see the tiled floor of the house. It is cut through by a gully where, it is supposed, a plaster and lathe dividing wall once stood. Continuing into the crypt allows us the chance actually to walk on another section of this second-century domestic floor. On the right are a number of artefacts belonging to the family which once lived here.

The plain red tesserae flooring, made of cubes of stone, was apparently a popular and hard-wearing floor at that time. Other examples, although not so perfectly preserved, may be seen beneath St Bride's church in Fleet Street and also in the nave of Southwark Cathedral.

Southwark Cathedral has other Roman remains to be seen. It was built on the site of either a home or possibly a temple. In 1977, a well was excavated beneath the cathedral and was found to contain a statue of a Roman-British cult figure: a hunter god accompanied by two dogs. He wears a Phrygian cap, giving him more than a passing resemblance to Mithras, the Persian god. This statue may be seen in the cathedral, next to a shaft which allows some of the archaeological excavations to be seen. A Roman coffin is on display here and also a section of the Roman road which passed through Southwark. Not far from here a temple complex was uncovered.

One of the almost unknown traces of Roman London is part of the basilica and forum which stood on Cornhill. This was the highest point in the city and therefore ideally suited for the most impressive building in the whole of Britain. The largest basilica north of the Alps and this gigantic, three-storey-high building combining law courts, government offices, market and shopping arcade, was visible across the whole of London. Today, Leadenhall market stands on the site, itself a little-known curiosity of nineteenth-century London. At the end of the market, at 90 Gracechurch Street, is a hairdresser's salon, Nicholson and Griffin. In the basement of this shop, protected by a glass window, is the only part of the basilica currently visible to the general public. There are other remains in nearby basements, but none that may be viewed freely. It is not necessary to have a haircut in order to see this last fragment of the basilica – the staff will cheerfully show it to casual enquirers.

The remains of two temples may be seen today. The most famous of these, the temple of Mithras, is in Queen Victoria Street, a stone's throw from the Bank of England. It was once on the bank of the River Walbrook, which flowed through the heart of Roman London. When this temple was uncovered in 1954, Londoners queued for hours to view the excavations. It was impossible to preserve it in place and so it was moved a few yards west to its present location. The way that it is now displayed, on a raised platform, is unfortunate. Mithraism was a mystery religion and the temples were gloomy and secretive places which were sunk into the ground. In plan, this temple is similar to a Christian chapel, with a columned nave ending in a curved apse.

A number of cult figures and other religious objects were found buried near the temple of Mithras and it has been supposed that these were hidden

in order to protect them from Christians who were intent on putting a stop
to the worship of Mithras. Moves are currently afoot during the redevelop-
ment of this area to return the temple to its original location on the bank of
the Walbrook. This scheme has been bedevilled by the competing rights of
the various freeholders of the office blocks around it and there seems to be
no clear idea of what is likely to happen in the end. At the time of writing,
the summer of 2011, it looks a little forlorn, standing as it does in the middle
of a building site.

The other Roman temple in London is a good deal harder to find than
the temple of Mithras, although no less accessible. It is to be found in
Greenwich Park, south of the Thames. One has to hunt around for this
tiny piece of history, although it is marked on the map of the park at the
entrance. Railings surround a block of masonry and mortar in which are set
the same red tesserae that we saw at Southwark Cathedral and beneath All
Hallows by the Tower. Excavations here unearthed the arm of a cult statue
holding a staff or bow. It is conjectured that this formed part of a statue of
Diana, to whom perhaps the temple was dedicated.

There are several well-preserved sections of the Roman city wall, apart
from those at which we looked near the amphitheatre. The largest and by
far the best preserved of these is to be found near Tower Hill tube station.
Nowhere can be seen to better advantage the building techniques used by
the Romans when undertaking this massive civil-engineering project.

Just outside the tube station at Tower Hill is a 20ft-high stretch of
London wall. Only the first 7ft or 8ft is Roman and it is worth going
right up to examine the structure of this part. Squared blocks of ragstone
are interrupted every yard or so by layers of tile. These were included to
provide stability and ensure that the courses of stone were completely
level. This stonework is still in perfect condition after 2000 years. Walking
round to the other side of this piece of wall is a grassy area and a little
park. The sheer size of the wall then becomes apparent. It is possible
to examine the building techniques used in the building of the wall by
looking at the ragged end nearest the Tower of London. This reveals
that the wall consists of two parallel walls built of shaped blocks. The
space between these two outer walls was filed with mortar and ragged
lumps of ragstone. A short walk from here are two other well-preserved
sections of the Roman wall. One is outside a hotel in Coopers Row.
This particular bit of the wall is worth examining if only to compare it
with the medieval wall built on top of it. The Roman wall is in perfect

condition after almost 2000 years. One feels instinctively that it could easily last another 2000 years. Not so the medieval section, which is a thousand years younger. This has the appearance of a crazy paving path, with irregular chunks of stone set any old how into mortar. Walking through a door in the wall gives one a good chance to examine the Roman section of the wall. From this side, the outer wall with its the sandstone plinth may be seen.

A few hundred yards north of here in the car park of an office is another bit of the wall. The foundations of a semi-circular bastion may be seen here, one of those added in the fourth century. These towers housed huge cross-bows called catapults, the artillery of their time. They were added in the fourth century, at a time when the city was thought to be threatened by Saxon invaders from the east.

Long after the original wall had been built to encircle the city, a river wall was also erected. This was in response to attacks from raiders who sailed up the Thames from the North Sea. It was not as methodically constructed as the city wall and there is evidence that different parts were put up on various different occasions. Some of it was very crudely built, with hardly any foundations. The only extant part of this river wall may be seen in the Tower of London. It is just inside the medieval curtain wall and consists of alternating courses of ragstone and tile.

Perhaps the earliest Roman remains which may be seen in London outside a museum are to be found in the porch of St Magnus the Martyr church in Lower Thames Street. It is a wooden beam from the first wharves which were established on the bank of the Thames in AD 70, only a decade or so after the complete destruction of the city by Boudica's forces.

One final piece of Roman London must be mentioned. This is the so-called London Stone, which is in Cannon Street. It has stood in this area for at least a thousand and probably closer to 2000 years. This small stump of limestone is behind a grill at No 111. Various legends have grown up about it. For instance, it has been claimed that it was an altar set up by Brutus the Trojan when he founded the city. More recently, it has been identified as the original stone from which King Arthur pulled the sword Excalibur. It is, however, more likely to be a fragment of Roman London. Some have claimed that it was a milestone, from which all distances to London were measured. There is little evidence for this and a more likely, if prosaic, explanation is connected with the stone's position. It lies just at the junction where the Walbrook

River enters the Thames. Near here, beneath Cannon Street station, was a civic building, perhaps the governor's palace in Londinium. It is likely that the London Stone is no more than a piece of the gate post from this building. It is easy to see how folklore would have grown up over the centuries, associating the governor's residence with power and authority. As the last surviving piece of this palace, the stone would be imbued with great significance.

It can be very hard when walking around modern London to appreciate the hills of the original city. So built up is the place now, that one can hardly notice where the hills were. A certain amount of effort is needed to get the feel of the topography of the city. The following walk, which covers a distance of 2 miles, will give readers a sense of the places at which we have been looking in this book.

We start at St Bride's church in Fleet Street. The basement of this church contains a stretch of red tesserae flooring from a Roman building. Since this location would have been not only outside the city wall, but also on the other side of the River Fleet, it would have been an odd place for a house. This was a sacred well and it is possible that a Romano-Celtic temple stood here, on the site of which a Christian church was later built. We leave the church and walk to Fleet Street. This was a Roman road called Akeman Street, which led from London to the West Country. Walk to Ludgate Circus and pause for a moment. We are now standing in the valley of the River Fleet. Looking up Fleet Street in one direction and Ludgate Hill in the other shows clearly that we are at the bottom of a valley. In Roman times a bridge crossed the river here. If you look to the left, you will see the bridge of Holborn Viaduct, which makes it clear that this is in fact a river valley. If we walk up Ludgate Hill, we are entering the Roman city; the gate was just where Old Bailey turns off on the left. We continue up the hill, which was one of the hills upon which the Roman city was built. When we reach St Paul's Cathedral, follow the line of the road round to the right of the cathedral as it becomes Cannon Street. Carry on, passing Carter Lane and Distaff Hill on your right. You have now passed the summit of Ludgate Hill and are heading towards the valley of the River Walbrook. When you come to a street called Friday Street on your right, turn into it and walk down to Queen Victoria Street.

Cross the road and turn left, walking along Queen Victoria Street. After a few yards, you will come to a tiny garden on the right and this is another part of Roman London. On this site stood the great public bathhouse of Huggin Hill. If you walk into the gardens, you will soon find that they drop steeply away in the direction of the Thames. One has a real sensation here of being on a hillside; not a common experience in this part of London. It is possible here to see a piece of Roman history of which few are now aware. Walk down the steps leading to a patch of grass. This overlooks the car park of an office block. To the left is a tangle of shrubs and ornamental plants. It is sometimes asserted that the remains of the Huggin Hill baths are no longer accessible to the public, but this is not strictly accurate.

The area in which you are standing is a bomb site. The remains of the Roman fort also lie in an old bomb site; a patch of ground where the Blitz destroyed buildings and exposed what lies beneath them. In the garden where we are standing, some of the walls which became exposed in this way are fairly modern – Victorian at the oldest. There are other, older walls, made of rougher, apparently hand-cast bricks. But there is something much older than this. If you pick your way carefully through the shrubbery and plants to the edge of the lawn, you can reach the farthest corner of the gardens. The wall here is very old, made of pieces of ragstone interspersed with Roman tiles. It is necessary to pull away the undergrowth to see this. However, beneath all this, right at the bottom, is the retaining wall of the Roman bathhouse. It is only a small section, but it is without doubt Roman stonework.

If you retrace your steps and continue walking along Cannon Street, away from St Paul's Cathedral, you will come to Walbrook Street on your left. The line of the River Walbrook runs parallel to Walbrook Street and crosses Cannon Street at this point. The dip in the road is quite clearly visible here. Carry on for a few yards and on your left-hand side you will see a grill set in a shop front. If you look through the grimy glass set behind this, you will be able to catch a glimpse of the London Stone, which we mentioned above. Across the road is Cannon Street station, the site of the civic building believed by some to be have been the governor's palace.

Continue walking along Cannon Street until you come to the Monument and then turn left and walk up Gracechurch Street. You are now walking up the hill upon which the original Roman camp was built during the Claudian invasion of AD 43. This is called Cornhill. You will come to the Leadenhall market, one of the lesser-known sights of the city – an iron- and glass-covered Victorian extravaganza. Stop for a moment and you are now standing upon the highest point in the city. It was here that the basilica and forum were built. If you want, you can now pop into the hairdresser at No 90, Nicolson and Griffith, and ask if you can see the base of the pier in their basement. This is a scheduled ancient monument.

The two museums in London to visit for anybody wishing to learn more about Roman London are the Museum of London on London Wall and the British Museum in Bloomsbury. The Museum of London has a large display covering every aspect of life in London at the time of the Romans. This consists of models of the city at that time and reconstructions of both shops and commercial premises. Many of the most important archaeological finds from the period are here, including the statues and sculptures from the temple of Mithras. The British Museum is concerned with Britain in general at the time of the Romans, although it too contains some finds from London itself. For example, there is a very fine mosaic which was found beneath the Bank of England. This has been on show in the museum for almost 200 years.

Appendix 1

The Chronology of Roman London

43   Claudius invades Britain and an army camp is established on the north bank of the Thames

47   Trees felled to make a wooden drain for the first street in London

50   Possible date for the construction of the first permanent bridge across the Thames at London

50   Possible date for the building of wooden quays and jetties

60   The destruction of the city by Boudica and her forces

61   Julius Alpinus Classicianus appointed procurator of Britain

70   Construction of first forum

90   Work begins on the building of the second forum and basilica. This takes 30 years to complete

100   Approximate date for the construction of a number of important buildings in stone, brought by river from Kent. These include the fort, amphitheatre and governor's palace

122   The emperor Hadrian visits Britain. His visit provides the impetus for new building work in the city

125   London ravaged by fire

165   The Antonine Plague sweeps across the whole empire. London's population declines and large parts of the city are abandoned

193   Clodius Albinus, governor of Britain, declares himself emperor and takes the army to fight in Europe

200   Approximate date for the building of London's wall. The fort is no longer used for military purposes after this time. Following the collapse of Clodius' attempt to seize the empire, Britain is divided into two. London is the capital now of only half the province, Britannia Superior

240	Possible date for the building of the Temple of Mithras
250	At about this time, a number of buildings west of the Walbrook are demolished. Main bathhouse also knocked down at about this time. Evidence that soil is brought in from outside the city in order to grow vegetables
280	Possible date for construction of part of the riverside wall to protect the city from attack from the water
286	Carausius lands in Britain and declares himself emperor. He makes London his base and sets up the city's first mint
293	Carausius murdered by Allectus, his financial advisor, who then assumes power
296	Constantius Chlorus invades Britain and overthrows Allectus, sailing up the Thames to save London from sack by rebel forces
367	The 'Barbarian Conspiracy' threatens London
375	Construction of bastions on east side of London wall
390	Riverside wall completed
406	British leader Constantine III takes the army to Europe and tries to seize the empire
408	The British expel Constantine's officials and sever links with the Roman Empire
409	Emperor Honorius tells the British that they must expect no further help from Rome. Saxon forces enter southern Britain
430	Romanised Celts still living in London and other walled cities of Britain
500	By this time London has been abandoned and lies in ruins

Appendix 2

Notable Characters from the History of Roman London

Julius Caesar (c. 101–44 BC)

Caesar came from an ancient and noble Roman family. He was a career politician and soldier who later became dictator of Rome. In 56 BC, he landed a Roman army in Britain and the following year returned with an even larger army and fought his way inland as far as Hertfordshire. His is the first written account we possess of that part of the Thames valley which would later become London.

Claudius (10 BC–AD 54)

Roman emperor from AD 41 until his death. His army invaded Britain in AD 43 and annexed it. A military camp was set up near a ford across the River Thames which later grew into the city of London.

Caratacus

A chief of the Catuvellauni tribe in Britain. After Claudius' invasion of his country, he fought a fierce guerrilla war against the Roman army until he was captured eight years later. In AD 51 he was taken to Rome as a captive, but his life was spared by Claudius. He was freed and allowed to settle in Rome.

Boudica

Wife of King Prasutagus of the Iceni tribe in Norfolk. On her husband's death she was badly treated by the Romans and launched an attack on the army of occupation. She and her followers destroyed Colchester, London and St Albans before being defeated in battle by the Romans. She was either killed or, according to some accounts, committed suicide in the aftermath of this defeat.

Suetonius Paulinus

Governor of Britain from AD 59. He launched a concerted attack on the Druid stronghold on the island of Anglesey off the coast of Wales. Later suppressed Boudica's uprising and beat her forces in a decisive battle. After her death, he punished the Britons by imposing a harsh military regime. This almost provoked another revolt and he was recalled to Rome.

Julius Alpinus Classicianus

Procurator of Britain from AD 61 until his death in AD 64. Of Celtic origin himself, he adopted a conciliatory attitude to the British in the wake of Boudica's revolt. He was responsible for the removal of Suetonius Paulinus, whose harsh methods disgusted him.

Vespasian Roman

Emperor from AD 69–79. As a young man, he fought in the invasion of Britain, spending some time campaigning in the country.

Agricola (AD 40–90)

Served in the Roman army of occupation in Britain under Suetonius Paulinus from AD 58 until AD 62. Later returned to the country as governor from AD 77 to AD 85. He was the father-in-law of the historian Tacitus, whose work is accordingly supposed to be informed by Agricola's reminiscences and official papers.

Tacitus (c.AD 55–120)

Roman historian whose works include the *Histories* and *Annals*. He also wrote a biography of Agricola which contains some of the earliest accounts of London.

Hadrian (AD 76–138)

Emperor of Rome from 117–138. Visited London in AD 122 and advised upon building works and defences. Instrumental in the building of Hadrian's Wall, the northernmost border of the empire.

Clodius Albinus (c.AD 150–197)

Governor of Britain from 192 until his death in 197. He declared himself Emperor of Rome and took the army in Britain across the channel to Gaul to fight the Septimus Severus, the generally accepted emperor.

Septimus Severus (AD 145–211)

Emperor of Rome from 193 until 211. In 208, Severus arrived in Britain with an army, intending to conquer Scotland. He was probably responsible for the walls which were built around London. He stayed in Britain for the rest of his life, dying in York.

Varius Marcellus

Appointed procurator in Britain from 197 by Septimus Severus.

Caracalla (AD 188–217)

Emperor of Rome from 209 to 217. Issued the *Constitution Antoniniana* in 212, which made all free men in the empire citizens of Rome. This had a great effect in provincial cities like London.

Carausius (AD ?–293)

Admiral in the Roman navy who seized control of Britain in 286, declaring himself Emperor of Britain and Gaul. The first man to establish a mint in London. He was murdered by his financial advisor, Allectus.

Appendix 2

Allectus (AD ?–296)

Ruled as Emperor of Britain and Gaul until his death in 296.

Constantius Chlorus (Constantine I) (AD 250–306)

Roman emperor from 293 until 306. He invaded Britain and deposed Allectus. By sailing a fleet up the Thames to London, he was able to save the city from the looting by mercenaries from the army of Allectus.

Constantine the Great (AD 272–337)

The son of Constantius Chlorus. Constantine was declared emperor at York in 306. At first, emperor only of Britain, France and Spain, he eventually took control of the whole empire.

Marcus (d. AD 407)

Leader of Britain and supposed emperor. Installed by the army in Britain and deposed and murdered by them a few months later.

Gratian (d. AD 407)

Declared emperor by the army in Britain and killed by them four months later.

Constantine III (d. AD 411)

Ordinary soldier who became leader of Britain from 407 until 411. He spent much time campaigning in Europe and, in his absence, the British decided that they wanted no more to do with the Roman Empire. Constantine's officials were ejected and from that time on London was the main city in an independent Britain.

Where to see Roman Remains in London

The Museum of London

London Wall
London
EC2Y 5HN
Tel: 020-7001-9844
Email: info@museumoflondon.org.uk
Open seven days a week, from 10 a.m. – 6 p.m.
Large gallery entirely devoted to Roman London. Contains many artefacts as well as reconstructions of full-size shops and domestic rooms. Also has a number of models, recreating the architecture of Roman London.

The British Museum

Great Russell Street
London
WC1B 3DG
Tel: 020-7323-8299
Email: information@britishmuseum.org
Open seven days a week, from 10 a.m. – 5.30 p.m.
A huge collection of Roman material from around the world, with special emphasis on this country.

The Amphitheatre

Guildhall Art Gallery
Guildhall Yard
London
EC2V 5AE
Tel: 020-7332-3700
Email: gallery@cityoflondon.gov.uk
Open Monday – Saturday 10 a.m. – 5 p.m. and Sundays 12 p.m. – 4 p.m.
The basement of the art gallery contains the remains of London's Roman
amphitheatre. A small exhibition details the discovery and preservation of
the amphitheatre, as well as giving some information about its history.

All Hallows by the Tower Church

Byward Street
London
Tel: 020-7481-2928
Crypt Museum open 10 a.m. – 5 p.m.
The crypt of this church contains the preserved remains of a second century
Roman house. Part of the red tesserae flooring has been preserved in situ
and it is possible to walk across it. There is also a display of items found from
this home. The crypt contains a large model of Roman London. Upstairs in
the church itself is the only remaining Saxon structure in London: an arch
built of Roman bricks and tiles.

Southwark Cathedral

London Bridge
London
SE1 9DA
Tel: 020-7367-6700
Email: cathedral@southwark.anglican.org
Open every day from 10 a.m. – 5 p.m.
The cathedral was built on the site of a Roman building and well. It is
possible that this was a temple. In the left aisle as one approaches the altar
is a section of red tesserae flooring from the Roman building beneath the
church. A shaft also allows one to see part of a Roman road; the only place

where one can actually see a Roman road in London. Nearby is a cult statue recovered from the well.

St Bride's Church

Fleet Street
London
EC4Y 8AU
Tel: 020-7427-0133
Email: info@stbrides.com
Open Monday – Friday, 9 a.m. – 5 p.m.
The church was built on the site of a Roman building. Flooring from this may be seen in the crypt, together with some parts of the walls.

The Temple of Mithras

The remains of this temple may be viewed at any time on the south side of Queen Victoria Street in central London. There is a question mark about their future location though, as it is hoped to return them to the bank of the River Walbrook, some yards to the south, where they were originally uncovered.

The Roman Fort

The foundations of two turrets of the fort and some of the walls may be seen in Noble Street, not far from the Museum of London. They are visible at all times. The west gatehouse of the fort lies beneath a car park. The museum of London, whose contact details are given above, arranges guided tours of the gatehouse once a month.

The London Stone

Behind a grill in the wall of a shop at 111 Cannon Street may be viewed a worn stump of limestone about the size of a microwave oven. This is the London Stone, about which many legends exist. It once stood on the other side of the road, closer to Cannon Street railway station. Since this was where the Romans had their central government offices, it is possible that the London Stone is a small part of the gateway of this building. It has been suggested that it is a Roman milestone, but there is no evidence either to support of disprove this contention.

London Wall

A number of well preserved stretches of the Roman city wall are still standing. Perhaps the most impressive is to be found right outside Tower Hill tube station. A little to the north at Coopers Row is another bit of the wall.

Wooden Post from the Roman Docks

In the porch of St Magnus the Martyr church in Lower Thames Street, is part of the wooden pilings for the docks built after the Boudican destruction.

Wall of a Bathhouse

At the junction of Huggin Hill and Queen Victoria Street, not far from St Paul's Cathedral, is Cleary Garden. At the far end of this garden on the leftmost point is part of the retaining wall of the main bathhouse for London. The bathhouse perched on this hill just above the Thames and this wall supported it.

The Remains of the Basilica

A number of shops and banks on Cornhill contain in their basements parts of the foundation and walls of the Roman basilica. The only piece of the basilica on public display is in the basement of Nicholson and Griffin. This is a hairdresser at 90 Gracechurch Street.

The Greenwich Romano-Celtic Temple

Perhaps the least impressive Roman structure in London is to be found in Greenwich Park. In a railed area is a chunk of masonry and mortar, in which are embedded a few red tesserae. It looks for all the world like an old chimney. This is all that remains of a temple to the goddess Diana which once stood here beside Watling Street. Colour Plate 16 shows how it would once have looked.

Bibliography

Alcock, Joan (1996) *Life in Roman Britain* London, B.T. Batsford

Bedoyere, Guy de la (2006) *Roman Britain: a New History* London, Thames & Hudson

Birley, Anthony (1964) *Life in Roman Britain* London, B.T. Batsford

Breeze, David & Dobson, Brian (1976) *Hadrian's Wall* London, Allen Lane

Caesar, Julius *The Gallic War*

Clayton, Antony (2008) *The Folklore of London* London, Historical Publications

———— (2000) *Subterranean London* London, Historical Publications

Cunliffe, Barry (1993) *The Roman Baths at Bath* Bath, Bath Archaeological Trust

———— (2010) *Druids* Oxford, Oxford University Press

Davies, Hunter (1983) *A Walk Round London's Parks* London, Hamish Hamilton

Delaney, Frank (1986) *The Celts* London, Hodder & Stoughton

Dyer, James (1990) *Ancient Britain* London, B.T. Batsford

Flanders, Judith (ed.) (1998) *Mysteries of the Ancient World* London, Weidenfield & Nicolson

Fraser, Antonia (1988) *Boadicea's Chariot* London, George Weidenfield & Nicolson

Frere, Sheppard (1967) *Brittania* London, Routledge & Kegan Paul

Glinert, Ed (2003) *The London Compendium* London, Allen Lane

Konstam, Angus (2001) *Historical Atlas of the Celtic World* New York, Checkmark Books

Matyszak, Philip (2003) *Chronicle of the Roman Republic* London, Thames & Hudson

Potter, David (2009) *Rome in the Ancient World* London, Thames and Hudson

Pryor, Francis (2003) *Britain B.C.* London, HarperCollins

Salway, Peter (1993) *A History of Roman Britain* Oxford, Oxford University Press

Sellar & Yeatman (1998) *1066 and all that* London, Methuen

Shuckburgh, Julian (2003) *London Revealed* London, HarperCollins

Smith, Stephen (2004) *Underground London* London, Abacus

Tacitus, translated by Harold Mattingly (1948) *Agricola* London, Penguin

Todd, Malcolm (1981) *Roman Britain 55 BC–AD 400* London, Fontana

Wacher, John (1978) *Roman Britain* Stroud, J.M. Dent

Williams, Brenda (2006) *Ancient Britain* Andover, Jarrold Publishing

Index